How to Make Your Own Web Site for the Older Generation

Other Books of Interest

*****

Acknowledgements

The author and publishers would like to thank Serif (UK) and Simon Monahan in particular for their help in the preparation of this book.

Also my son David Gatenby for his help with the research and production of this book and my wife Jill for her forbearance throughout the project.

How to Make Your Own Web Site for the Older Generation

Jim Gatenby

BERNARD BABANI (publishing) LTD
The Grampians
Shepherds Bush Rd
London W6 7NF
England

www.babanibooks.com

Although every care has been taken with the production of this book to ensure that any projects, designs, modifications and/or programs, etc., contained herewith, operate in a correct and safe manner and also that any components specified are normally available in Great Britain, the Publishers and Author do not accept responsibility in any way for the failure (including fault in design) of any project, design, modification or program to work correctly or to cause damage to any equipment that it may be connected to or used in conjunction with, or in respect of any other damage or injury that may be so caused, nor do the Publishers accept responsibility in any way for the failure to obtain specified components.

Notice is also given that if equipment that is still under warranty is modified in any way or used or connected with home-built equipment then that warranty may be void.

© 2006 BERNARD BABANI (publishing) LTD

First Published - April 2006

British Library Cataloguing in Publication Data:

A catalogue record for this book is available from the British Library

ISBN 0 85934 610 2

Cover Design by Gregor Arthur

Printed and bound in Great Britain by Cox and Wyman Ltd

About this Book

Your own Web site is an enjoyable way to share your latest news, information and photographs, etc., with family, friends or business contacts wherever they are in the world.

This book attempts to show that anyone can create a personal Web site easily and cheaply; it's no longer a specialized task requiring technical know-how. Thanks to the development of easy-to-use software you don't need to program the computer in the special HTML language used by Web pages. Much of the software is provided free online – and so is the Web space needed to host your site.

The book starts with an introduction to Web sites and explanations of the essential Internet jargon that cannot be avoided. This is followed by descriptions of the various methods of establishing a Web presence; these are arranged in a progression, starting with the simple "blog" or online diary, where you just type text into a preformatted page.

Next you are introduced to an online Web page builder, Yahoo! GeoCities, which provides free software tools and step-by-step guidance, enabling anyone to get a Web page on the Internet in minutes. Another chapter explains how a familiar word processor such as Microsoft Word can be used to produce perfectly adequate Web pages.

Next a dedicated Web design program, Serif WebPlus, is described in detail, covering all aspects of Web design and management to produce a fully-featured Web site.

Final chapters show how to publish your new Web site on the Internet and how to prepare your digital photographs for use in Web pages and in an online photo album.

Serif WebPlus Software Offer

Readers can obtain a substantial discount on the Serif WebPlus software described in this book. Please see page 181 for details.

About the Author

Jim Gatenby trained as a Chartered Mechanical Engineer and initially worked at Rolls-Royce Ltd, using computers in the analysis of jet engine performance. He obtained a Master of Philosophy degree in Mathematical Education by research at Loughborough University of Technology and taught mathematics and computing to 'A' Level for many years. He has written over 20 books in the fields of educational computing and Microsoft Windows, including several of the highly successful "Older Generation" titles from Bernard Babani (publishing) Ltd.

The author, himself a member of the "over 60s club", has considerable experience of teaching students of all ages, in school and in adult education. For several years he successfully taught the well-established GCSE and CLAIT Computing and Information Technology courses.

Trademarks

Microsoft, MSN, Hotmail, Windows, Paint, FrontPage, Word, Works, Internet Explorer and Windows are either trademarks or registered trademarks of Microsoft Corporation. Paint Shop Pro is a trademark or registered trademark of Corel Corporation. Adobe Photoshop and Adobe Photoshop Elements are trademarks of Adobe Systems Incorporated. WebPlus is a trademark or registered trademark of Serif (Europe) Ltd. Google and Blogger are trademarks or registered trademarks of Google Inc. Yahoo! and GeoCities are trademarks or registered trademarks of Yahoo! Inc. LiveJournal is a trademark or registered trademark of LiveJournal.com. CuteFTP is a trademark or registered trademark of GlobalSCAPE. Photobucket is a trademark or registered trademark of Photobucket.com Inc. All other brand and product names used in this book are recognized as trademarks or registered trademarks, of their respective companies.

Contents

4

5

6

7

8

9

Introducing Web Sites

Creating a Personal Web Site

It's never been easier to publish your own Web site on the Internet, whether you create a simple page of news and pictures or a site covering several feature-packed pages.

Nowadays you no longer have to write instructions in the special HTML format used by the Web; there are lots of easy-to-use software tools that have turned Web site creation into a task similar to word processing.

This book describes several easy and inexpensive methods of establishing a personal Web presence:

- The online diary or "blog" enables you to enter text and pictures simply into a ready-made format.

- The photo album displays your latest pictures online to a worldwide audience of friends and family.

- The Web page "wizard" guides you through the process of replacing the content in professionally designed templates to make your own Web pages.

- A familiar word processor, such as Microsoft Word can be used to produce finished Web pages.

- A dedicated Web design program, like Serif WebPlus, can be used for the creation and editing of a sophisticated Web site with many special features.

If you already have a computer connected to the Internet, most of the work described in this book can be carried out using free software and free Web storage space.

Making Good Use of a Personal Web Site

Once you have created a Web site and installed it on the World Wide Web, it is then accessible to <u>millions</u> of people anywhere in the world – all they need is a computer with an Internet connection and a Web browser such as Internet Explorer. Here are some typical uses of Web sites:

- Displaying the latest family news and information including text, photographs and audio and video clips. The information can be viewed by friends and family wherever they live in the world.

- Providing an up-to-date, interactive, newsletter or magazine for a club, village or local community. Housebound people can participate from home.

- Advertising a small business and obtain orders from around the world. No other medium can access such a large market so easily. Forms can be provided on the Web site for taking orders and obtaining payment. Latest information can be updated in minutes and is then instantly available worldwide.

- Sharing your experiences and expertise with a world-wide audience. This might involve a hobby such as rebuilding a classic car or reviews of holidays, music, books or the theatre.

- Posting information that might be helpful to others, perhaps based on your experience of dealing with serious illness or personal misfortune. This could be in the form of an online diary, now more commonly known as a *blog*, an abbreviation for *Web log*.

The Main Parts of a Web Page

Shown below is the first page of a Web site involving Peak District walks. The main features of the page are numbered and these are described in detail below.

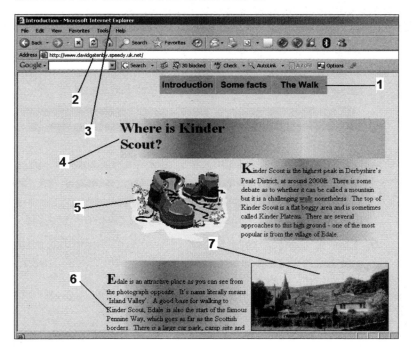

1 This is the *navigation bar*. In this example the navigation bar consists of 3 clickable *links* or *hyperlinks* that are used to launch each of the pages on the Web site. The navigation bar appears on every page on this particular Web site, permitting movement between Web pages in both directions.

Introduction   Some facts   The Walk

2 This is the unique address of the Web page, known as the URL or Uniform Resource Locator, discussed in more detail later.

Address 🛰 http://www.davidgatenby.speedy.uk.net/index.html

3 The name of the Web browser program that is being used to display the Web site on the Internet, in this case the popular Microsoft Internet Explorer.

🛰 **Introduction - Microsoft Internet Explorer**

4 The heading for this particular page, entered in a separate text frame, enabling the heading to be moved and formatted independently.

5 This is a piece of artwork or "clipart" supplied with the Serif WebPlus software package that was used to create this particular Web site.

6 The main body text, like the heading is entered in its own text box, allowing independent formatting and editing.

7 A photograph taken with a digital camera, transferred to a computer and inserted into the Web page. This topic is discussed in more detail later in this book. For more information on digital photography, please also see Chapter 9, Working with Photographs.

Web Pages are Easy to Create

None of the methods of creating Web pages described in this book are difficult or require technical experience. However, some of the methods are more involved than others because they allow you to incorporate more features into your Web pages. Therefore the book has been structured, as far as possible, to allow the reader to make steady progress while working sequentially through the chapters. The methods described are:

- The online diary or "blog" and online photo albums
- The online Web page builder using wizards and ready-made templates
- Creating Web pages using a word processor – Microsoft Word
- The use of dedicated Web design software (Serif WebPlus).

These methods are briefly outlined below and discussed in more detail in the remainder of the book.

The Online Diary or "Blog"

This is one of the easiest ways to get a Web presence. The task is reduced to simply typing in a daily journal. All of the formatting, i.e. page layout, etc., is done for you and you can choose from a number of ready-made page designs. You don't need to worry about transferring your blog pages onto the Internet – the program takes care of everything. You can insert pictures as well as text and you finish up with a Web address that other people can use to connect to your blog. Here they can view your pages and add comments. Similarly the online photo album is also very simple to create and this is discussed in detail in Chapter 9, Working with Photographs.

1   Introducing Web Sites

The Online Web Page Builder

This is more versatile than the blog. Online page builders
such as Yahoo! GeoCities described in this book provide
all of the tools needed to create a Web page. You can
choose from a range of ready-made templates and themes
as shown in the small sample below.

Sanrio Themes - Choose Hello Kitty or Badtz-Maru templates from Sanrio.

Blue Angel   Flowers & Frills   Badtz-Maru

In GeoCities, under the control of the page wizard, you
replace the default text and pictures with your own page
content, using a "painting by numbers" approach. All work
is carried out online so you don't have to worry about
uploading your pages to the Internet.

Using a Word Processor to Create Web Pages

A word processor such as Microsoft Word can easily be
used to create a Web site. First you open a new blank Web
page, enter text and pictures in the normal way, before
saving the page in the HTML format used for Web pages.

Save as type: Web Page (*.htm; *.html)

A **Web Page Preview** option on the Word **File** menu enables
the page to be checked in a Web browser such as
Internet Explorer. A tool to create hyperlinks, as
shown on the right, is also provided on the word
processor toolbar.

Using a Web Page Design Program

This is a program specifically designed for the creation, management and editing of multiple-page Web sites. Serif WebPlus has been used as the basis of this section of the book because it is very easy to use yet powerful enough to produce any sort of personal Web site. There are also very good help facilities and tutorials.

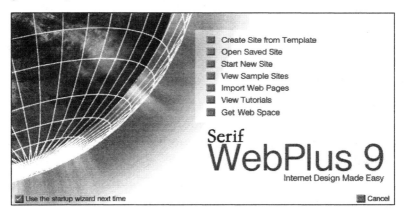

This type of software allows you to build a multi-page Web site with a consistent page layout, based on master pages providing a background to every Web page. There are many other features including ready-made page templates, colour schemes, artwork and sound and video clips.

Programs such as WebPlus have built-in facilities for transferring Web pages to the Internet; this is simpler than using a separate file transfer program as required for pages produced in the word processor, for example.

All of these methods of creating Web sites are discussed in more detail in the rest of this book.

Essential Web Terms Explained

The next few pages introduce some of the main features of the Internet and the World Wide Web.

The Internet

The Internet consists of millions of computers around the world. These computers are able to communicate with each other via telephone, cable and satellite networks. Apart from e-mail, communication includes the exchange of files of various types such as Web pages, which can contain text, pictures, music and video clips. The computers on the Internet include those used by individuals, mainly for obtaining information and sending e-mail messages. These computers are known as *Web clients*. The powerful computers provided by Internet companies to store Web pages accessible to the whole world are known as *Web servers*.

When you are "surfing" the Internet and click a link to another Web page, a copy of the page is fetched from the server storing the page. The Web page is then *downloaded*, i.e. copied, to your computer.

World Wide Web

This is a set of linked pages of information, accessible to anyone with a computer, an Internet connection and a program called a *Web browser*. Sir Tim Berners-Lee, a British scientist, was the inventor of the World Wide Web, a means of communicating information between different computers using linked pages. A popular Web browser is Microsoft Internet Explorer; this is used to display Web pages and to navigate between different pages on millions of computers around the world.

Web Page

A Web site consists of one or more Web pages. The Web page is created in a special format known as HTML as discussed below, which is quite different from the format of a normal document produced, for example, in a word processing program. An important feature of the Web page is the insertion of links or hyperlinks to move to other Web pages and also to other Web sites.

A Web page can include pictures as well as multimedia objects such as sound and video clips and animated graphics. Most multi-page Web sites designate the first or introductory page as the Home Page.

HTML

This stands for Hypertext Markup Language and consists of a set of commands used to specify how the text and graphics are laid out on a Web page. Early Web sites were constructed by manually typing in HTML instructions, using instructions such as **<h1>** for a heading size and **<center>**, for example. Nowadays it's possible to create Web pages without knowing anything about HTML, thanks to the development of dedicated Web page creation software which produces the HTML code for you.

Professional Web designers still write their own HTML instructions to fine-tune the code produced by software packages such as Microsoft FrontPage or Macromedia Dreamweaver. Learning HTML is time consuming but not difficult; if you really have the time and inclination to get into the "nuts and bolts" of Web pages there are lots of books on the subject.

Link (also known as a Hyperlink)

A link is a special piece of text or a picture which, when clicked, fetches and displays another Web page. The new page may be on the same

Return to Jim's Home Page

Web site as the page containing the link or on another Web site on a server computer anywhere in the world. When you let the mouse pointer hover over a text link or a picture which has been set up as a "clickable link", the pointer changes to a hand. Also when the pointer is over a text link, the text appears underlined, as shown in the link above.

As discussed later, text and pictures can easily be made into clickable links using Web page creation software.

URL (Uniform Resource Locator)

In the same way that every house has its own address, every Web site has a unique address, known as a URL. Entering the URL into the address bar of a Web browser such as Internet Explorer takes you straight to the home page of the Web site. A fictitious URL is shown below:

http://www.mywebsite.co.uk

Domain Name

The part of the address to the right of **www.**, i.e. **mywebsite.co.uk** in the above example, is known as the *domain name*. You can make up your own domain name and register it with a specialist company, for a small annual fee. In the above example the *extension* **co** denotes a company Web site and **uk** is the country. If someone else has already registered your first choice of domain name you can either make up a new domain name or use a different extension. There are many other extensions available, as discussed later.

Web Server

This is a special computer used to store Web pages and exchange information over the Internet. Many servers are located at the Internet Service Providers (ISPs) like AOL. Subscribers to an Internet Service Provider may be allocated some free space on a server, enough to store a small Web site. Alternatively, a Web site may be stored on a server belonging to a *Web host*, as discussed below.

Web Host

Web hosts are companies who usually charge a monthly premium to allow you to store your Web site on their server. Small Web sites are sometimes free, although in this case you might have to tolerate a lot of advertising.

Web Client

A Web client is one of the millions of computers used by individuals to "surf" the Internet and obtain information from the World Wide Web.

Downloading

This is the process of copying information (files, Web pages, etc.) from a Web server computer down to a *client* computer used by an individual in their own home, school, college, business or office, etc.

Uploading

This involves copying Web pages and other files from a client computer up to a Web server; here they are saved and are then accessible to millions of users around the world.

FTP Client

A special program that uses a system known as **File Transfer Protocol** for uploading Web pages to a server.

Who Will See Your Web Site?

1. Tell People the Address of Your Web Site

If you have created a Web site intended for friends, family or colleagues to view, you need to tell them the URL or address of your site. Then they enter the address in a Web browser such as Internet Explorer as shown below. On clicking the **Go** button or pressing the **Enter** key, your home page should open up almost immediately.

You could send an e-mail to all of your contacts, containing the address of your Web site. The address can be in the form of a "clickable link" to your Web site, embedded within the text of the e-mail. If you have any business cards or stationery, your Web address could be printed on them.

2. Finding Your Site as a Result of a Search

Your Web site may be listed in the results of a search using Google, for example. Clicking your address in the results list launches your home page.

3. Links from Other Sites

You can arrange to have links to your Web site included in other Web sites. This would be particularly helpful if you have friends or associates involved in related activities or businesses, just as, for example, airline Web sites have links to hotels, car hire, etc.

The Stages in the Creation of a Web Site

The following are the main stages in the creation of a Web site, although not always in the order shown below.

Planning

Make a rough plan of the site including sketches of the home page and links to the other pages. Consider your target audience as this will influence the style of the pages. You will also need to decide the content including the text and any pictures or photographs, etc.

Preparation

Gather together on your computer all of the photographs, artwork, files, etc., and save them in a single folder on your hard disc. Photographs can be edited by "cropping" to make them smaller or converted to "thumbnails "for faster loading – discussed in more detail later.

Creating the Web Pages

Use the Web creation software to construct the Web pages, including the text, navigation bars, links to other pages and any embedded photographs, pictures or other features. Initially the Web pages will be created, tested and saved locally on your own home or office computer. The pages can then be uploaded and saved on a server computer, giving worldwide access. Alternatively you might use one of the online page builders like Yahoo! GeoCities in which tools are provided to allow you to create your Web pages.

Obtaining a Domain Name

Identify a name for your Web site that has not been used by anyone else. Register the name, for a small annual fee. Your Internet Service Provider or Web host might arrange the domain name for you.

Finding a Home for Your Web Site

You will need to find space for your Web site on a server computer at your Internet Service Provider or Web hosting company. This may be either free or require a monthly premium and may also allow several e-mail addresses.

Publishing Your Web Site

When you have completed your Web site on your own computer, it can be tested to make sure the various links work. Then it is "uploaded" to the Internet and saved on the Web server space which you have previously arranged. All of the other files (such as photographs, etc.) are uploaded at the same time.

Promoting Your Web Site

You need to publicise your site to friends, relatives, etc. Methods are available to make it more likely that people will find your site when surfing the Internet. You may be able to arrange for your site to be connected to other sites by the inclusion of clickable links on each site.

Maintaining Your Web Site

From time to time you will need to amend the pages of your Web site, e.g. to reflect news or changed circumstances or to correct errors. For example, if you are running a small business your prices may change; obviously a newsletter or magazine Web site will need updating with each new edition. The Web site can be updated by amending the pages on your local (home) computer then uploading them to the Web server, as discussed in detail later in this book.

What Do You Need to Get Started?

The following items are needed to get started on creating your own Web site; detailed information about each topic is given later in this book.

A Computer with a Connection to the Internet

You need a modern computer such as a "PC" type machine running the Microsoft Windows XP operating system. A device called a *modem* provides the physical connection to the Internet. If possible obtain one of the latest *broadband* connections as this is much faster for sending and receiving information. Check with your telephone or cable network company for the availability of broadband in your area.

Space on a Web Server for Your Web Site

An Internet Service Provider such as AOL, for example, provides your connection to the Internet via one of their servers. They usually charge a monthly subscription and this may include some Web space for storing your own Web site. If your site is likely to grow you may need to buy a greater amount of server space from a special Web hosting Company.

Software for Creating Web Pages

You can use a word processor to produce Web pages, although better results can be obtained using dedicated page creation software known as an *HTML editor*. Some companies provide *online software* for building Web sites, including ready-made *templates*. Well-known online software includes the Yahoo! GeoCities PageBuilder. Software for preparing Web sites on your own computer (prior to uploading to a server) includes Serif WebPlus, Microsoft FrontPage and Macromedia Dreamweaver.

A Digital Camera

This will enable you to take
photographs and store them on your
computer. Then they can be edited,
ready for incorporating into a Web
page.   Software   for   editing
photographs and preparing them for
the Web may be provided with a new camera. The
Microsoft Office suite of software includes the Microsoft
Photo Editor program. Otherwise, popular software for
editing photographs includes Adobe Photoshop Elements
and Paint Shop Pro.

A Scanner

You   may   have   some
photographs in the form of
prints that you wish to include
in a Web page. A scanner will
allow you to convert the print
into digital form so that it can
be saved on your computer.
Then it can be edited, saved
and incorporated into a Web page.

The preparation of digital photographs for use in Web
pages is discussed in more detail in Chapter 9, Working
with Photographs. Further information on the subject can
also be found in my earlier book:

Digital Photography and Computing for the Older
Generation from Bernard Babani (publishing) Ltd.

Keeping an Online Diary or "Blog"

Introduction

Later chapters in this book show how you can unleash your creativity to design your own Web site from scratch. However, one of the quickest and easiest ways to establish a Web presence is to set up a special sort of site called a *blog* (short for *Web log*). This will allow you to place text and pictures on the Internet in no time at all. Then family and friends (or anyone else) anywhere in the world can read your thoughts in the form of a diary or journal. The process is made easy by special online software which reduces the task to a simple typing operation. All of the trickier jobs, such as setting up the page layout and *uploading* your words of wisdom to the Internet, are done automatically by the software – it couldn't be easier.

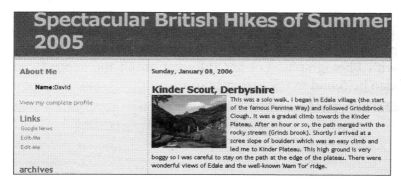

Spectacular British Hikes of Summer 2005

About Me

Name: David

View my complete profile

Links

Google News

Edit-Me

Edit-Me

archives

Sunday, January 08, 2006

Kinder Scout, Derbyshire

This was a solo walk. I began in Edale village (the start of the famous Pennine Way) and followed Grindsbrook Clough. It was a gradual climb towards the Kinder Plateau. After an hour or so, the path merged with the rocky stream (Grinds brook). Shortly I arrived at a scree slope of boulders which was an easy climb and led me to Kinder Plateau. This high ground is very boggy so I was careful to stay on the path at the edge of the plateau. There were wonderful views of Edale and the well-known 'Mam Tor' ridge.

What is a Blog?

A blog is really a special type of Web site and is simply an on-line diary or journal. The author of a blog records regular entries on a particular subject of interest, so that it can be read by a worldwide audience. Like a diary, it is written in an informal tone and may include photographs. It is common for a blog to have links to other relevant Web sites. You can also allow readers of the blog to add or "post" their comments to the blog page.

Some possible topics for a blog might include:

- Ongoing family news including photographs.
- An account of an epic journey.
- A dispute, for example a proposed new housing development or motorway.
- Progress following a new diet.
- Dealing with a serious illness.
- A journal describing a series of regular trips in pursuit of a hobby, such as bird watching.
- Keeping an ongoing record of important current affairs, such as the pensions crisis.
- Settling into a new community at home or abroad.

As there is little or no censorship over the content of Web pages, it is possible for the blog facility to be abused. As discussed later, if you find someone else's blog offensive it's possible to record or *flag* your objections. If enough people complain, the providers of the blog facility may take some appropriate action.

Software for Creating and Updating Blogs

A blog could, in theory, be written on a word processor like Microsoft Word. The page would consist of a list of dates with a paragraph and possibly a picture against each date. The page would be saved as an HTML file (as discussed earlier) and uploaded to an Internet Server so that a large audience could see it. Using specially-designed blog software, however, it's much easier to create a blog without any specialist knowledge of Internet technology. It's just a case of typing into the simple word processor provided in the blog software. However, unlike the word processor, your blog thoughts can potentially be shared by millions of people. Also, if you choose to allow it, readers of your blog will be able to interact with you. The blog software takes care of the whole process, including storing your pages on the Internet.

While software to create an ordinary Web site can cost between £50 and £300 or more, software to set up a blog is very cheap or free of charge. Before using the software you will need to complete some registration formalities, as shown for the LiveJournal blogging community below.

Key Features of a Blog

- A blog is an online diary or journal.

- Everything you need is usually free and provided online – there's no need to buy expensive software.

- Numerous ready-made templates are available at the touch of a button, to give a stylish, well-designed appearance to your pages.

- Text is entered into an easy-to-use built-in word processor with full editing and formatting features.

- Dates are added automatically as sub-headings.

- Pictures already stored on your hard disc can be uploaded and inserted into a blog. The software makes this an easy task (as discussed later).

- Links to other Web sites can be inserted into a blog.

- The blog continually grows as you make new daily entries or *posts*.

- You can choose to invite or reject comments about your blog from people who have read it.

- A blog is created online. This means your work is immediately saved on a Web server computer and is then available for the whole world to see.

- Users of popular software packages such as Blogger or LiveJournal are part of a community of hundreds of thousands of bloggers.

- While using the blogging software, links to other blogs are displayed on the screen. Click on a few of these links to have a look at the rants and raves of bloggers all over the world.

Blogger

This is a very popular and easy-to-use program and has been around for several years, having been created in 1999 at Pyra Labs in San Francisco.

Shown below is the opening screen from the popular **Blogger** program. This software is free and available online at the **Blogger** Web site.

www.blogger.com

Once online you can start using the program immediately. Online software such as this is run directly from the Internet – you don't need to obtain a CD and copy it onto the hard disc sitting inside of your computer. Any text or pictures which you enter into your blog are saved immediately on the Internet.

Starting Your Own Blog

Once you've decided upon a suitable subject to write about, you're half way there. Entering the Web address **www.blogger.com** will take you to the **Blogger** site. This includes explanatory notes such as **What is a blog?** and **TAKE A QUICK TOUR**, which outlines the main features of the program. Apart from the main function as an online diary and forum for discussion, you can also use Blogger to display and share photographs. Text and photos can be sent from a mobile phone and "posted" to your blog page. To have a look at other people's blogs, the **Explore blogs** feature on the **Blogger** startup screen displays links to newly updated blogs created by other people. This list changes constantly.

As shown on the right of the screen below, **Blogger** helps you to create a new blog in just three easy steps.

This program is really user-friendly and it only takes a few minutes to set up your diary. To get started, click **CREATE YOUR BLOG NOW** as shown on the previous page.

The first task is to **Create an account**, by making up and entering your username and password. These can be any words of your choice.

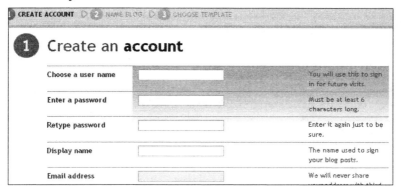

Now enter a **Display name** as shown above; this is your name as the author and this will be displayed on the blog. After entering your **Email address**, the next screen, **Name your blog** enables you to give your blog a title.

Type in the name of your blog in the **Blog title** bar as shown above. Then enter a **Blog address (URL)**. Here you enter any word of your choice and Blogger creates a web address for you. This will enable other readers to find your blog and read it. **Word Verification** is a security feature which requires you to type in the characters that appear in the picture.

The final preparation stage is to select **Choose a template** from the Blogger startup screen shown earlier.

There are currently twelve templates to choose from. You can preview a template and it's possible to choose a different template later if you change your mind. Click on your chosen template then click **CONTINUE** at the foot of the page. Blogger then creates your blog, a process only taking a few seconds.

You will then be presented with the following screen – at this stage there is no text or pictures in your blog, it's just an empty shell.

The process of entering text and pictures into a blog and saving them on the Internet is known as *posting*. Now click on **START POSTING**. This takes you to a word processor screen into which you can type the text of your blog.

You are now ready to begin blogging.

Enter a heading relating to the current day in the **Title** bar at the top of the page. The current date will be added automatically later on when the blog is published.

As shown above, this screen has all of the main text formatting features of a word processor, including various fonts (styles of letters), bold and italic effects, bullets, numbered lists and a spelling-checker. There are several other important tools on the Blogger creation or *posting* screen shown above. For example, clicking **Post and Comments Options** near the bottom left of the screen presents the radio buttons shown below. These enable you to **Allow New Comments on This Post**. (Or disallow comments by clicking **No** if you prefer).

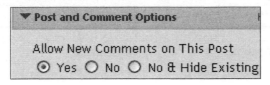

Inserting a Link into a Blog

The main screen for entering the text of your blog, as shown on the previous page, contains an icon for inserting a link into a blog page. This icon is shown on the right.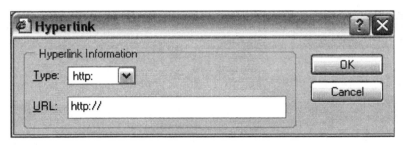

Such links (or *hyperlinks* to use the full jargon) enable visitors to your blog to connect to other relevant Web sites. When you click the link icon, the following dialogue box appears, allowing you to enter the name of the relevant Web site in the **URL** bar.

Then click **OK** to finish creating the link.

Inserting a Picture into a Blog

An icon is provided on the top of the posting screen to allow you to insert a picture or photo, etc.

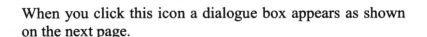

When you click this icon a dialogue box appears as shown on the next page.

The **Browse** button shown on the left below allows you to search for pictures that have been stored in a folder on your hard disc. This will need to be copied to Blogger using the **Upload Image** button shown below. Then it will be available to other Internet users. You can also copy a picture from another Web site if you know the address or **URL** where it is stored. Enter the address in the **URL** bar shown on the right of the screen below.

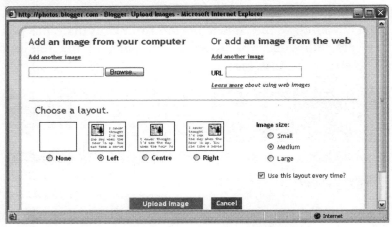

The **Choose a layout** and **Image size** features shown above allow you to set the position of the picture on the blog page and also specify its size, i.e. **Small**, **Medium** or **Large**.

When you click **Browse** the **Choose file** dialogue box opens allowing you to select the folder containing the required picture or image. Then click **Open** and **Upload Image**. You are told that the image is being uploaded to the Blogger server on the Internet and finally you see the message **Your image has been added**.

Click **Done** to see your blog with the picture inserted as shown below.

Once you are happy with the text and any pictures it's just a matter of clicking the **Publish Post** button, as shown above. The following reassuring message should appear.

Your blog is now available on the Blogger Web site **www.blogspot.com** for anyone to view. Click **Sign out** when you wish to end the session.

Viewing and Editing an Existing Blog

Each time you enter some text and post it as previously described, it is added to your blog with the current date and time automatically inserted. To make additional entries or posts to a blog, start Blogger by entering **www.blogger.com** or by adding blogger to your list of **Favourites**. The Blogger startup screen appears, as shown earlier in this chapter.

Enter your Blogger **Username** and **Password** and click the **SIGN IN** button as shown above. This opens up the Blogger dashboard, as shown below.

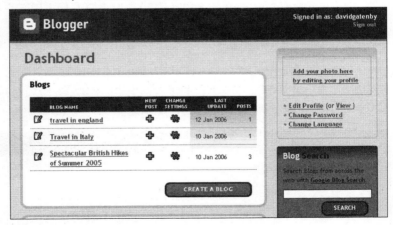

The **Dashboard** lists all of your blogs as well as various Blogger news and information items and a list of other people's **Blogs of Note** for you to view. There are also links to the ten most recently updated blogs.

If you click on an entry for one of your blogs in the **Dashboard** shown on the previous page, the next screen shows all of the posts in the blog.

This shows that the selected blog, **Spectacular British Hikes of Summer 2005** has three posts. As shown above, there are buttons to **Edit** each individual post or **View** or **Delete** the post. (One post is similar to one day's entry in a traditional diary in book form). The **View Blog** tab shown above displays the entire blog as it will appear to other users on the Internet.

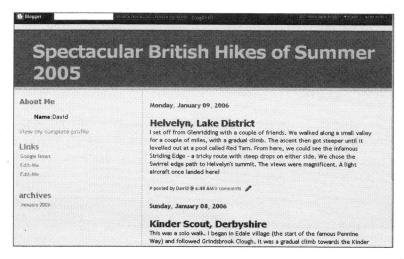

As you can see from the extract from the blog on the previous page, the layout is uncluttered and user-friendly. The left-hand side shows links to other Web sites; you can catch up on the latest **Google News** in addition to reading the blog as shown on the right. Across the top of the screen is a small menu, also known as a *navigation bar* shown below.

The **NEXT BLOG** option takes you to a blog written by someone else on another subject altogether.

An important feature in the navigation bar is the **FLAG?** facility. Since blogging allows people to express their personal views, there is always the possibility that a blog may be offensive in some way. After all, a blog can be used as a "soapbox" for anyone in the world to rant and rave about their favourite likes or dislikes. If a reader finds the content of a blog offensive, they can inform Blogger of this by clicking on the **FLAG** button. Should there be sufficient complaints made by other people, then Blogger will take the necessary action, perhaps adding a warning to the blog or removing it from the Blogger listings.

The **GET YOUR OWN BLOG** option shown above allows you to return from someone else's blog to one that you have created.

The left-hand side of the Blogger navigation bar includes two **Search** buttons, enabling you to either search for key words within your current blog or search the Internet for blogs on a particular subject.

SEARCH THIS BLOG on the previous page enables you to look for words in the blog you are reading, by entering key words in the search bar. For example, entering **Kinder** in **SEARCH THIS BLOG** produced the following result:

Should you wish to read from a much earlier date then click **archives** lower down the screen then select the appropriate month.

SEARCH ALL BLOGS allows you to look for key words in blogs anywhere on the Internet, including those written using different software and by different authors. When **Grindsbrook,** for example, was entered in a **SEARCH ALL BLOGS**, the following results appeared.

Creating Another Blog

If you are already signed on to Blogger and wish to start a completely new blog, there's no need to go through all the initial signing on procedures as described earlier. Instead you simply select **CREATE A BLOG** from the **Dashboard** screen shown earlier. This will take you to the **Name your blog** screen as described previously. Fill in the details as before, choose your template then start typing in the text of your first post to the new blog.

Promoting Your Blog

If you want to promote a blog to a wider audience, click on your blog title in the **Dashboard** screen. The following screen will appear, from which you select the **Settings** tab, as shown below.

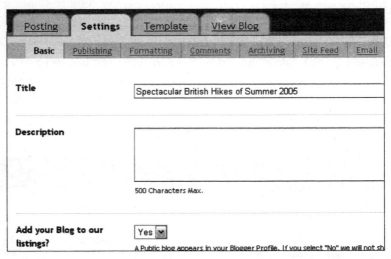

On the dialogue box shown above, answer **Yes** to the question **Add your Blog to our listings?** Other Blogger users will now be able to view your blog.

Allowing Others to Add Comments

Moving along the navigation bar on this tab, you will see a **Comments** option. Selecting this will reveal the screen as shown below.

Who Can Comment? Allows you to restrict comments to certain users or alternatively allow anyone to comment.

There are several radio buttons giving options for the way comments from readers are handled in Blogger. For example, selecting **Yes** on the **Comment Moderation** option allows you to view the comments before they appear on your blog. Then you can either approve or reject the comment.

Useful Web Sites Involving Blogs

There are now thousands of Web sites giving information about blogs and help with their creation, as well as directories with clickable links to thousands of blogs. The list of addresses below is far from exhaustive but should enable you to read the thoughts of many people around the world and perhaps enter into a meaningful dialogue. Simply type the address into your browser such as Internet Explorer and press **Enter** or click the **Go** button.

www.weblogs.co.uk   www.typepad.com

www.blogger.com   www.livejournal.com

www.movabletype.org   www.blogwise.com

www.blograma.com   www.getblogs.com

Shown below is an extract from the **Getblogs** directory, which has links to thousands of blogs in different categories, as well as a **Blog Directory Search** feature.

3

Creating a Web Page in GeoCities

Introduction

Yahoo! is one of the major providers of news and information on the Internet, with extensive directories and search facilities. GeoCities is a Yahoo! Web site which provides all of the tools needed to create your own Web site online, i.e. while you are connected to the Internet. This is one of the quickest and easiest ways to create a personal Web site – a Web page can literally be online in minutes. Some of the main features of GeoCities are:

- A range of packages costing various amounts, from a free Web page carrying advertising to subscription packages having more facilities and no advertising.

- Your own Web address, user ID and password.

- A PageWizard which guides you, step-by-step, through the process of building a Web page.

- A choice of Web page templates which can be customized to include your own text and pictures.

- Web page creation software allowing you to design and create your own site starting from a blank page.

- Software and tools provided free online – all you need is a computer and Internet connection.

Getting Started with GeoCities

Log on to the Yahoo! site at **www.yahoo.com**. This opens up the main Yahoo! Directory, shown below, with a link to GeoCities on the left-hand side.

GeoCities   Clicking the **GeoCities** link on the left opens up a welcome screen. This includes links to pages giving details of the various GeoCities packages – **Free**, **Plus** and **Pro**. If you click the link **Learn more** you can take the **Yahoo! GeoCities Tour**, which goes through the various steps in creating and publishing a Web site with **GeoCities**.

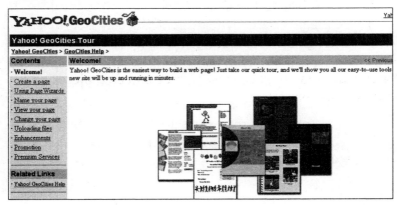

The PageWizard

The GeoCities tour explains that there are two basic ways of creating Web pages, the **Yahoo! PageWizard** and the **Yahoo! PageBuilder**.

The PageWizard "holds your hand" while you customize a ready-made template with your own words and pictures, using an approach similar to "painting by numbers".

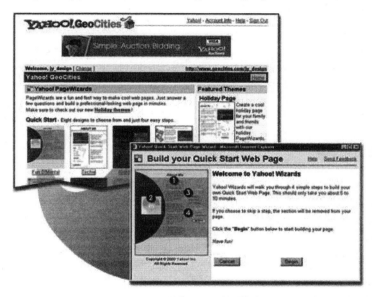

Each of the pieces of text (or pictures) in a Web page template are numbered. Under the guidance of the PageWizard, you replace each of the numbered pieces with your own text or picture.

The PageBuilder

The PageBuilder puts the user more in control of the process of creating a Web page. You can start off with a blank page and enter your text and pictures from scratch; or you can customize one of the many Web page templates provided. With the PageBuilder, the text and any pictures in a template are replaced in any order, not in a numbered sequence as in the case of the PageWizard.

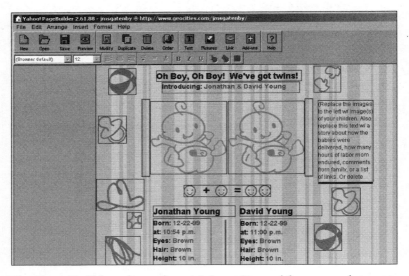

The PageBuilder above has a Menu Bar with a complete set of tools for creating and editing Web pages, also shown below, presented here in two halves for the sake of clarity.

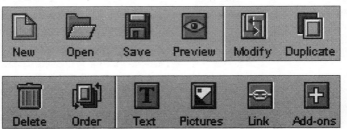

Signing up to GeoCities

The first step in creating your own Web page is to set up an account with GeoCities, after clicking **Sign Up** on the **Welcome** screen shown earlier. If you sign up for the **FREE** package you can always upgrade later to one of the GeoCities subscription packages, **PLUS** or **PRO**. After clicking **Sign Up**, you then complete a registration form with your full name, etc. At this stage you make up your own **Yahoo! ID** and **Password**. If your chosen **ID** has been taken, GeoCities suggests variations that are still available. For example, **jamesgatenby** was already taken but the suggestion **jmsgatenby** was still up for grabs.

YAHOO! GEOCITIES

Already have an ID or a Yahoo! Mail address? **Sign In.**

Fields marked with an asterisk * are required.

Create Your Yahoo! ID

* First name:

* Last name:

* Gender: Male

* Yahoo! ID:
ID may consist of a-z, 0-9 and underscores.

* Password:
Six characters or more; capitalization matters!

* Re-type password:

Yahoo! Mail: ☑ Create my free Yahoo! email address.
Your address will be the ID you've chosen follow

An additional security requirement in the GeoCities registration is the selection of a **Security question** from a drop-down menu; you then enter your own answer to this question. The security question will allow you to get online to GeoCities even if you forget your password.

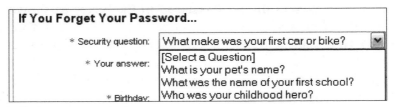

After entering your date of birth and either accepting or declining the chance to receive marketing information, you type in a verification code. This consists of several special characters displayed in a slightly jumbled fashion in a box on the screen. The security code is intended to prevent automated registrations from clogging the system. If you now click a box to agree to the terms of the registration, a **Registration Completed** form is displayed confirming all of your details, such as your Yahoo! ID, e-mail address and security question. You are advised to print this form. Finally you are sent a confirmation e-mail, including a link which has to be clicked to activate your new account.

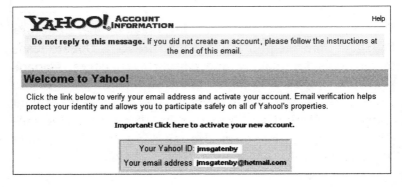

Signing in to a GeoCities Account

Now you can sign in to your account in GeoCities. Enter **www.yahoo.com** into the address bar of your Web browser such as Internet Explorer. Next select **GeoCities** from the directory, as shown near the beginning of this chapter, and enter your **Yahoo! ID** and **Password** in the boxes as shown on the right below.

A screen showing the **GeoCities Control Panel** opens up; this contains a navigation bar with links to the main sections of the GeoCities Web site, as shown below.

The **Home** button above includes links to the **GeoCities Tour** and other helpful information. **Create & Update** leads to the tools for making and editing Web pages. **Manage** helps you upload Web pages and files, including images, to the Internet. A **Site Status** panel records the amount of your allocated 15MB disc space that has been used. **Promote** displays links to Web sites offering to increase the number of visitors to your site, using various strategies.

Creating a Web Page With the PageWizard

Click **Create & Update** on the **Control Panel** shown on the previous page. The following window is included on the screen which appears.

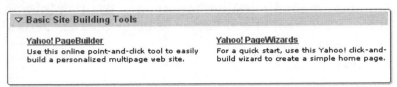

The GeoCities **PageWizard** is one of the easiest and quickest ways to get your own Web page online and this is discussed in the rest of this chapter.

(The **PageBuilder** can be used to create a Web site from a blank page. This topic is covered using various software packages later in this book.)

Now click **Yahoo! PageWizards** as shown above. You are presented with eight **Quick Start** designs; later these can be customized by inserting your own text and pictures.

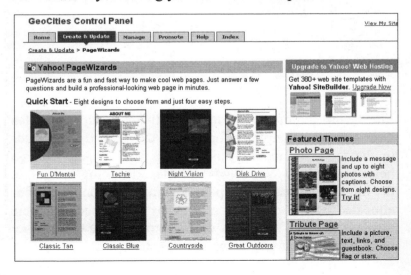

There are also several more specific template themes; a small sample of these is shown below.

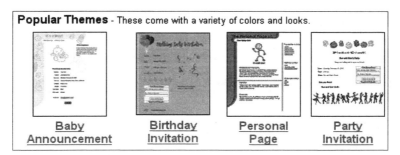

When you have chosen a template, select **Create new page** and then choose from a number of styles including different colour schemes and layouts.

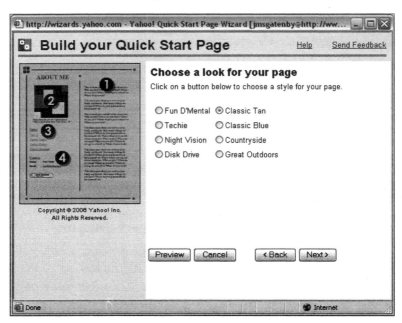

Entering the Text in the PageWizard

After you click **Next**, it's time to start work by entering a title for the Web page and replacing the text provided with your own content.

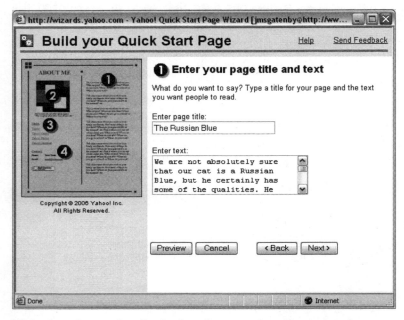

This is where the "painting by numbers" comes in; you enter the text in the box provided; the number on the main panel on the centre right of the page above corresponds to a number on the miniature Web page shown on the left-hand side. As shown above, you can also enter a page title.

Click the **Preview** button shown above to see what your Web page will look like when it is displayed in a Web browser such as Internet Explorer. You can view your page in the Web browser by clicking the **Preview** button at any stage of the creation process in the PageWizard.

Inserting a Picture in the PageWizard

After you have entered the text for the column headed **1** on the previous page, clicking **Next** moves on to the picture, **2**. To use one of your own pictures in GeoCities, it will need to be uploaded from your hard disc to your account at the GeoCities Web site. To do this select **Upload new image...**, as shown below. (If you have already uploaded some pictures to GeoCities, you can select **Choose One** to use a picture from your online account).

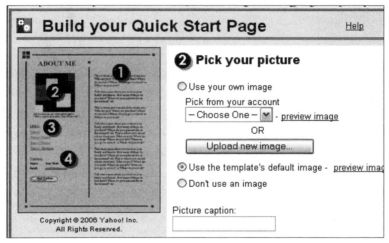

If you select **Upload new image...** you then click **Browse** to find the picture you require by searching through the folders on your hard disc. This is done using the **Choose file** dialogue box shown on the next page. Please note that a **Picture caption** can be added at this stage as shown above.

Before starting work on a Web page, it's a good idea to prepare any pictures and store them in a known location, i.e. folder, on your hard disc, as discussed in detail later in this book.

Click the down arrow to the right of the **Look in:** bar to open a drop-down menu and start looking for the folder containing the required picture.

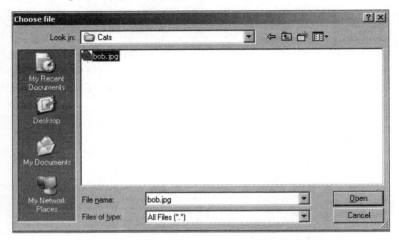

Once you have browsed and found the picture you want to insert in your Web page, click **Open**. The path to the picture **C:\Cats\bob.jpg**, in this example, appears in the **Upload Image** window as shown below.

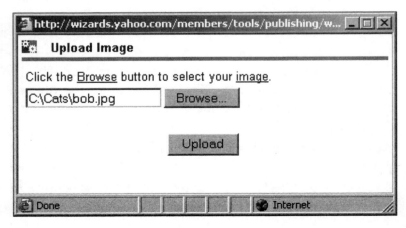

Now click the **Upload** button shown on the previous page to copy the picture up to your GeoCities account. The PageWizard informs you that it's sending the image and asks you to be patient. Once the picture has been successfully uploaded it can be selected from your GeoCities online account, as shown below.

On clicking **Next**, the picture is inserted into your Web page in place of the default picture. Click the **Preview** button to see how the picture will look in a Web browser such as Internet Explorer.

Adding Links to Your Web Page

The next dialogue box, shown below, asks you to enter your favourite links to allow visitors to your site to connect to other relevant Web sites.

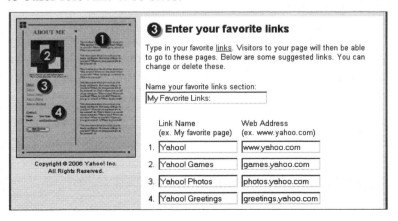

You can, if you wish, use some or all of the Yahoo! links provided. These include the **Yahoo! Photos** which enables you to create an online photo album. Online photo albums allow you to display your photographs to a worldwide audience and are discussed in more detail later in this book.

Yahoo! Greetings provides electronic messages to send to your friends and relatives. To have a look at the Yahoo! links in action, click **Preview** shown above. This displays your Web page in the Internet Explorer. Click any of the links to find out more. Some of the facilities provided on the Web sites accessed by these links require a subscription.

Alternatively, you may wish to enter some links of your own, as shown in the (fictitious) examples below:

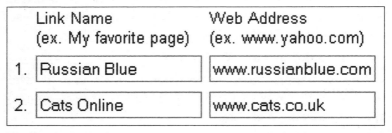

	Link Name (ex. My favorite page)	Web Address (ex. www.yahoo.com)
1.	Russian Blue	www.russianblue.com
2.	Cats Online	www.cats.co.uk

On clicking **Next**, the final stage is to enter contact details such as your name and e-mail address, before entering a name for the page. There is also an option to place an **I'm Online** button on your Web page inviting people to send you an e-mail message, after clicking the button.

After clicking **Next** you are asked to **Name your page,** as shown below. This becomes the last part of the Web address of the page.

Lastly a **Congratulations!** window appears giving the address of the new GeoCities Web site.

http://www.geocities.com/jmsgatenby/mypage.html

Click this link to open the new Web page. You now have a Web site on the Internet which can be viewed by friends and relatives anywhere in the world.

Visitors to your site simply enter your Web address into the **Address** bar of their Web browser, such as Internet Explorer, and up pops your Web site, as shown below.

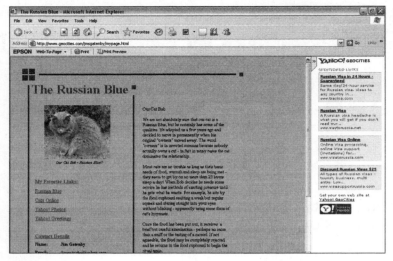

As this is a free Web site, advertisements appear under **SPONSORED LINKS** down the right-hand side. These all relate to the word **Russian** used in the title of this example.

In the Web address shown below, the part to the right of **www**, i.e. **geocities.com/jmsgatenby**, is known as the *domain name*.

http://www.geocities.com/jmsgatenby/mypage.html

mypage.html is the name of this particular Web page. If a Web site consists of several pages, the first page visitors encounter is known as the Home Page. This is given the special name **index.html**, rather than **mypage.html** in the simple example above. Then you make up relevant names for the other pages and add the extension **.htm** or **.html** (either may be used).

Creating Web Pages With a Word Processor

Introduction

Most of us now have a word processor such as Microsoft Word or Works, which can be used quite easily to create a Web site consisting of text and pictures. Both Word and Works allow documents to be saved in the HTML format used by Web pages, as shown below.

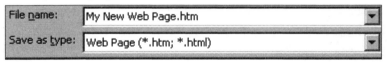

In addition, the Word and Works word processors have a tool for inserting *hyperlinks*; these are the clickable pieces of text or pictures which enable anyone surfing the Internet to move to different Web pages or different Web sites. Word also includes a Web Page Wizard which helps to automate the construction of a Web site and there are ready-made Web page templates in Word which can be adapted to make your own pages.

Although the work in this chapter is based on Microsoft Word, the general ideas apply to most word processors. (Microsoft Word is supplied both separately and as part of the Microsoft Works Suite integrated software package).

If you are already familiar with a word processor, such as Word or Works, which allows you to save pages in the HTML format, this is a very cheap and easy way to create a Web site. You don't have to invest money on a new piece of software or spend hours learning how to use it.

When you have completed the entry of text and any pictures, etc., and saved the pages in the HTML Web page format, the site must be *uploaded* or copied to the Internet. Before you can do this you will need to arrange for a company known as a Web host to provide space on their Web servers. These are special computers which enable Web sites to be viewed on the Internet by a worldwide audience. These topics are discussed in more detail in a later chapter in this book, Publishing Your Web Site.

If you use one of the dedicated Web creation programs such as Serif WebPlus, Microsoft FrontPage or Dreamweaver, the program has a built-in feature for uploading Web pages to a Web server. When using a word processor like Word or Works, it is necessary to use a separate program called an *FTP client*, such as CuteFTP. This can be downloaded free from the Internet. Uploading Web pages in CuteFTP is discussed later in this book in the FTP section of the chapter Publishing Your Web Site. This task is not difficult – it amounts to "dragging and dropping" your Web document files from a screen panel representing your own (local) hard disc to another panel representing the remote computer belonging to the Web host. To upload any Web sites to a server you will need:

- An account with a Web host
- The address of their FTP server
- A username and password.

Creating a Simple Web Site in Word

The next few pages show how a simple Web site can be constructed in Microsoft Word. Although it only consists of two linked pages, the same methods can be used to create a site of any number of pages.

The **Dove Valley Gardeners** Home Page shown below online in Internet Explorer was created in Microsoft Word and uploaded to a Web host using the FTP client CuteFTP.

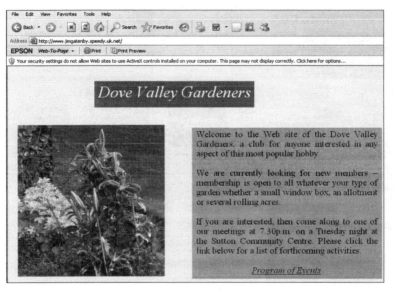

Before starting on the actual Web page, it's a good idea to create a new folder for the site using the Windows Explorer. Right-click the **Start** button and select **Explore**. Now click and highlight the **C** drive and select **File, New** and **Folder**. Replace the words **New Folder** with the name of your Web site, **Dove Valley** in this particular example.

Gather together any pictures needed and put them in the new Web site folder. In this example, the required picture, **pink lily** is in the folder **Garden** and needs to be copied to the new Web site folder **Dove Valley**. This can be done in the Windows Explorer using "drag and drop" with the right-hand mouse button held down, then selecting **Copy** from the menu which appears when you release the button. Alternatively select the photo **pink lily** and click **Edit** and **Copy** and then select the folder **Dove Valley** and click **Edit** and **Paste**.

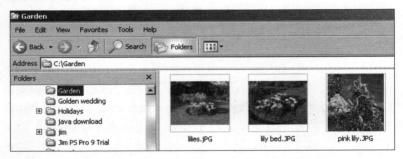

Now the new Web site folder **Dove Valley** contains the picture **pink lily** as shown below.

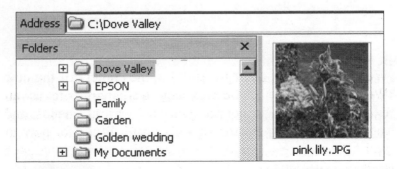

The Web pages for the site will also be saved in this folder.

Switching to **View** and **Details** in the Windows Explorer shows (in the extract below) that this picture, **pink lily**, is a **JPEG Image** file, occupying some **801KB**. These facts are mentioned because the type and size of picture files have a significant effect on the performance of Web sites; this subject is discussed in more detail later in this book.

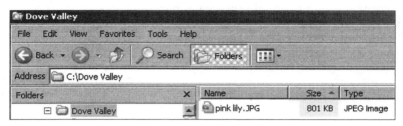

Starting a New Blank Web Page

From the Word Menu Bar select **File, New..., General Templates** and **Web Page**. You are presented with a blank page and you will see that the **New Blank Document** icon under **File** on the Menu Bar has changed to the **New Web Page** icon, shown on the left and below. This can be used to insert additional Web pages.

We are now ready to begin entering the content of the new Web site, using the **Dove Valley Gardeners** site as an example. The skills needed and the various menus and tools are exactly the same as when using Word for normal word processing – one of the advantages of this approach to Web page creation.

Working With Text Boxes

It's a good idea to enter different paragraphs, titles and blocks of text in *text boxes* – these are easy to move about and can also be formatted separately. This means you can change the font style, text size and background and foreground colours, etc., of just a small block of text.

To insert the heading **Dove Valley Gardeners**, click **Insert** and **Text Box** off the Word Menu Bar and drag out the text box to roughly the right size. The text box can always be resized later by dragging on any of the eight small squares on its perimeter.

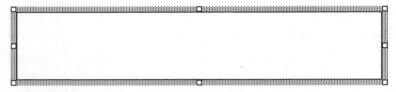

The text box can be moved after placing the cursor on one of the edges so that it changes to a cross with four arrow heads. Now the text box can be dragged to any position.

Enter the text for the title, such as **Dove Valley Gardeners**. You can set the font style and size before you begin typing; alternatively type the text in the default size and style then highlight the words by dragging the cursor over them with the left-hand mouse button held down. Now use the Word toolbar to select the style and size of letters and any formatting effects such as italics, centred text, etc.

In the title **Dove Valley Gardeners** the **Times New Roman** font was used in size **28** points and italics.

Changing the Text or Font Colour in a Text Box

You will probably want to enhance your text boxes with colour. To change the colour of the text you must first highlight the text by dragging the cursor over it as mentioned earlier. Then select **Format** and **Font...** from the Menu Bar and click the down arrow below and to the right of **Font color:** as shown below.

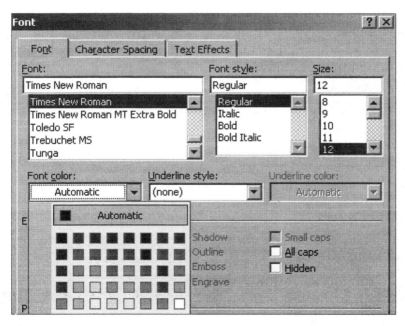

Select the colour for your text then click **OK** and then click outside of the text frame to remove the highlighting.

Changing the Background Colour in a Text Box

To fill a text box with colour, select the text box so that the eight small squares appear on its perimeter. Now select **Format** and **Text Box...** from the Word Menu Bar and the **Format Text Box** window appears as shown below. Make sure the **Colors and Lines** tab is selected.

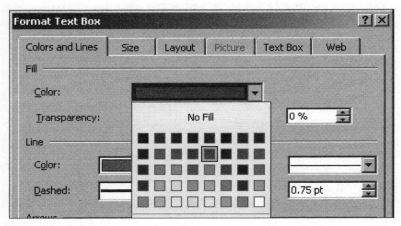

Click the down arrow to the right of **Fill** and **Color:** and choose the colour for your background from the drop-down colour chart. Click **OK** and then click outside of the text box to deselect it. The heading for the Home Page of the simple **Dove Valley** Web site is shown below.

Dove Valley Gardeners

The **Text Box** dialogue also allows you to select, under **Line** shown above, a border in various styles and thicknesses.

Changing the Background Colour of the Entire Page

A background colour for the entire page, excluding any text frames or pictures, etc., is applied after selecting **Format** and **Background** from the Word Menu Bar. As soon as you click a colour on the grid, as shown below, the new background colour is applied to the entire Web page.

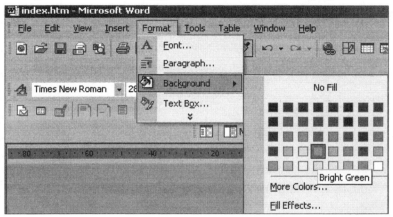

If you click **Fill Effects...** shown above you can select and apply a **Texture** and **Pattern** for the Web page background.

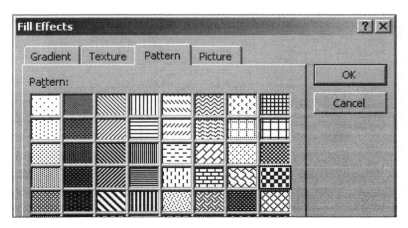

Inserting a Picture into a Web Page

As mentioned earlier, it's essential to have any pictures needed for your Web site in a folder where you can find them easily. In this example, the picture **pink lily** has already been saved in the folder for the new Web site, **Dove Valley**.

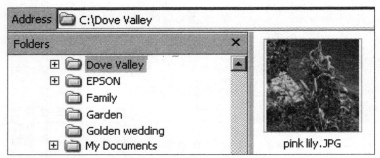

To insert the picture onto the Web page, from the Word Menu Bar select **Insert**, **Picture** and **From File**.... Click the down arrow to the right of **Look in:** shown below and browse to find the folder containing your required picture.

Now click **Insert** to place the picture on the Web page. Before you can (easily) resize and move the picture it's necessary to format the picture. Click over the picture and eight small squares appear around the perimeter. Now click **Format** and **Picture....** From the **Format Picture** dialogue box, select the **Layout** tab as shown below. Now click **Behind text** and **OK**. You can also select **Left, Center** or **Right** under **Horizontal alignment.**

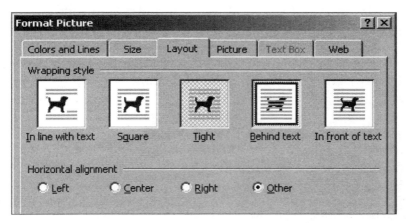

Resizing a Picture

The picture should now have eight circles around its perimeter. Drag any of the corner circles (which change to double arrows) to resize the picture.

Moving a Picture

Apart from the **Horizontal alignment** feature shown above, the picture can also be moved after clicking, i.e. selecting it, so that the eight circles appear on its perimeter. Then allow the cursor to hover over the edge of the picture so that the cross with four arrows appears. You can now drag the cross to move the picture in any direction.

4   Creating Web Pages With a Word Processor

The work in this chapter so far has covered the following:

- Opening a new blank Web page in Word.
- Inserting text in a text box, formatting with different fonts and foreground and background colours.
- Applying a background colour and patterns to an entire Web page.
- Resizing and moving a text box.
- Obtaining a picture from a folder on the hard disc and inserting into a Web page. Moving and resizing the picture.

The above skills are sufficient to produce the simple **Dove Valley Gardeners** Web page shown below.

Although not described in this chapter, the right-hand block of three paragraphs shown above was created and formatted in a text box in the same way as the title box. This was described earlier in this chapter. We now need to consider saving a Web page, creating additional Web pages and linking them with clickable hyperlinks.

Saving a Web Page in a Word Processor

You should save your work regularly – a power cut or other disaster can easily destroy hours of work. The first page on the **Dove Valley** site was intended as the Home Page. This is the page normally seen first by visitors when they arrive at your site. The Home Page typically welcomes visitors, indicates the contents of other pages and provides clickable links to the other pages. It is normal for the Home Page on any Web site to be given the special name **index.htm**. Other pages can have any name you choose, although they always end in the extensions **.htm** or **.html** (either can be used).

When your Web page is complete, from the Word Menu Bar select **File** and **Save As**....

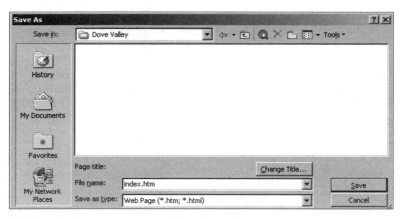

Click the down arrow to the right of **Save in:** and browse to find the folder for your new Web site, in this case **Dove Valley**. Make sure the **Save as type:** bar is showing **Web page (*.htm: *.html)**. Enter the name **index.htm** in the **File name:** bar and click the **Save** button to place a copy of the Home Page on your hard disc.

After you have saved your first Web page it will appear in the Windows Explorer in your chosen folder, as shown below for the **Dove Valley** example.

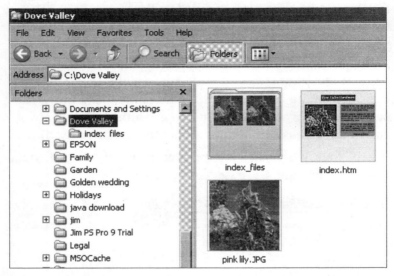

The extract above was taken from the Windows Explorer after selecting **View** and **Thumbnails**. You can see that, apart from the original picture file, **pink lily.JPG**, we have the Home Page **index.htm**, complete with a miniature version of the page. In addition Word has automatically created an extra folder, **index_files**. This latter folder contains a file list and low and high resolution copies of the **pink lily.JPG** image.

Inserting Another Web Page in Word

As Word is operating in Web page mode, the normal **New Blank Document** icon under **File** on the Menu Bar has been replaced by the **New Web Page** icon as discussed earlier in this chapter. Click this icon to insert a new blank Web page.

Now enter the text and any pictures for the second page, such as the **Events** page in the **Dove Valley** Web site, shown below. The text is entered in text boxes and formatted using the same methods as described earlier for the Home Page.

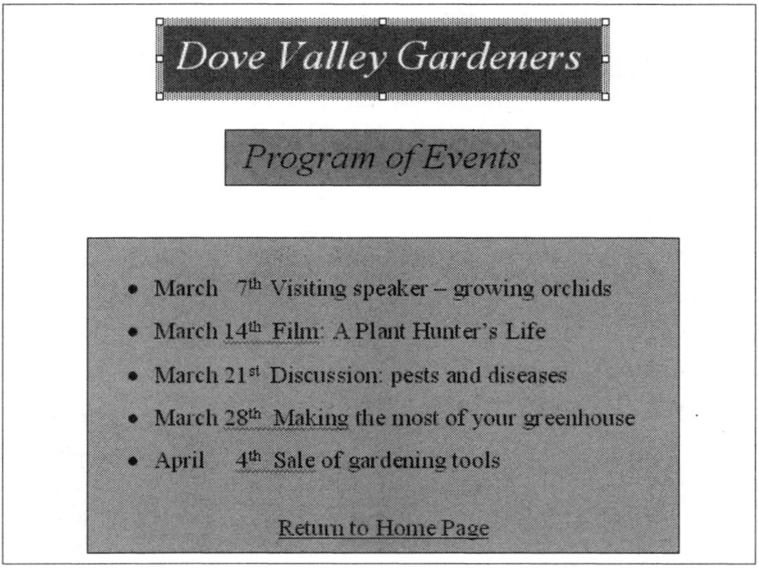

Dove Valley Gardeners

Program of Events

- March 7th Visiting speaker – growing orchids
- March 14th Film: A Plant Hunter's Life
- March 21st Discussion: pests and diseases
- March 28th Making the most of your greenhouse
- April 4th Sale of gardening tools

Return to Home Page

When the text has all been entered and the various foreground and background colours applied, the second Web page can be saved using **File** and **Save As...**, as described earlier.

The second page is again saved as a Web page in the **Dove Valley** folder with **events.htm** as the **File name:** in this particular example.

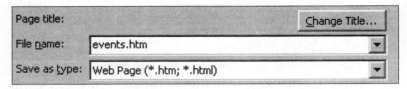

The folder for the Web site, **Dove Valley** in this example, now has all of the necessary files for the two pages, including one photograph.

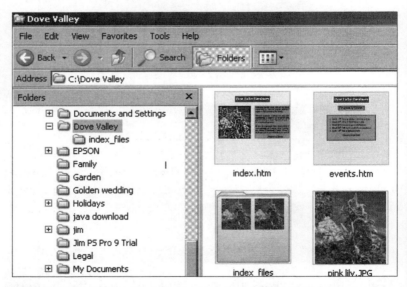

This simple Web site, stored in the folder **Dove Valley** on the hard disc in my computer, now consists of two Web pages, **index.htm** and **events.htm**, shown above. In addition the folder contains the original picture **pink lily.JPG** and a folder, **index_files**, which Word has created automatically.

Inserting Hyperlinks

One last task remains before the Web site is uploaded to the Internet. We need to insert some links or hyperlinks to allow movement between Web pages and to connect to other Web sites if necessary.

The Web site **Dove Valley** has two pages, **index.htm** and **events.htm**, as shown below. We need to make some clickable links to allow movement between the two pages in both directions.

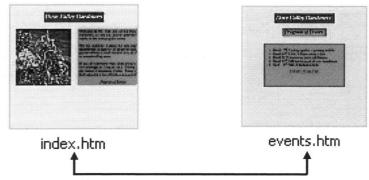

index.htm   events.htm

Open the first page **index.htm** in Word and insert the text for the link to the second page, such as ***Program of Events*** shown below. Now highlight this text by dragging over it with the cursor, with the left-hand button of the mouse held down.

If you are interested, then come along to one of our meetings at 7.30p.m. on a Tuesday night at the Sutton Community Centre. Please click the link below for a list of forthcoming activities.

Program of Events

Right-click over the text for the link and select **Hyperlink...** from the menu which appears. Alternatively click the **Insert Hyperlink** icon, shown on the left. The dialogue box, **Insert Hyperlink**, opens as shown below.

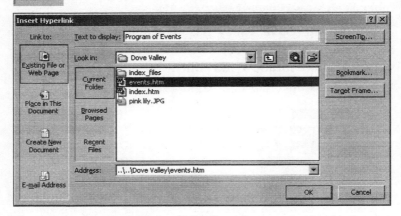

The text to be used as the link already appears in the **Text to display:** bar shown above. Otherwise you can enter or edit the text at this stage. In this example, the Home Page is to be linked to the second page, **events.htm** stored in the same folder, **Dove Valley**. Therefore we select **Current Folder** as shown above. The centre panel should now display all of the pages of the Web site. Click on **events.htm** in the centre panel and the path to this Web page should now appear in the **Address:** bar as shown above. After you click **OK** the text in the link appears underlined.

Please note that the **Insert Hyperlink** dialogue box shown above also allows links to be made to other Web sites. In this case the full Web address or URL (**HTTP://www.** etc.,) of the remote site must be placed in the **Address:** bar shown above. A link to a recently visited Web site can be made after clicking **Browsed Pages**, shown above.

The same method can be used to create a link from the **events.htm** page to return to the Home Page, **index.html**.

- April   4th Sale of gardening tools

Return to Home Page

Using a Picture as a Hyperlink

A screen object such as a picture or photograph can be used as a hyperlink. Right-click over the picture, etc., as before for a text link, and then select **Hyperlink...** from the menu which appears. Alternatively, click to select the picture or object and click the **Insert Hyperlink** icon, shown on the left, from the Word Menu bar. The **Insert Hyperlink** dialogue box opens as shown earlier and the link is created as before for the text-based link.

Previewing Your New Pages in Your Web Browser

You can check the way your Web pages will appear on the Internet by previewing them in a Web browser such as Internet Explorer. From the Word Menu Bar select **File** and **Web Page Preview**. The preview is carried out *offline* – at this stage the Web pages have not been uploaded to the Internet. In the preview, make sure the hyperlinks work correctly to open the required pages or files; when you pass the cursor over a hyperlink it should change to a hand.

After testing the site in your Web browser, return to the word processor to carry out any editing resulting from the preview. Then preview the site again and continue this process until you are satisfied with the Web site. Make sure the Web pages are all saved in the **.htm** format.

Uploading a Web Site to the Internet

This topic is covered in more detail in the chapter, Publishing Your Web Site, later in this book. However, a brief overview of the process is given here.

Web sites produced in a word processor like Microsoft Word are uploaded with a special *FTP client* program, such as CuteFTP, downloadable free from the Internet. You will need to obtain Web space for your site from your Internet Service Provider or a Web hosting company. They will also arrange with you a **username** and **password** and give you the address of their FTP server. This is the Internet computer that your files will be copied to.

The procedure is to start up the FTP client program, such as CuteFTP, on your computer, then connect to the FTP server of your Internet Service Provider or Web host. In CuteFTP, shown below, the left-hand panel shows the files in the Web site folder on your computer. The right-hand panel represents the remote computer of the Internet Service Provider or Web host. The Web site is uploaded to the Internet by dragging the files from the left-hand panel to the right-hand panel, using the mouse.

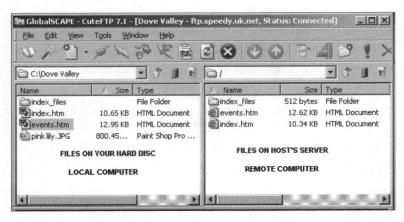

The Web Page Wizard in Microsoft Word

This facility allows you to create a Web site in Word using a host of ready-made features. A wizard is a program that leads you step-by-step through a process, offering you a number of choices at each stage, before you click **Next** to move on to the following stage. The wizard is in complete contrast to the "blank canvas" approach, where you type in all of the contents from scratch on a blank page. The **Web Page Wizard** in Word allows you to:

- Create a Web site with any number of pages

- Set up a horizontal or vertical navigation frame with clickable links providing movement between pages

- Insert, remove and rename Web pages

- Use ready-made Web page templates which can be adapted by inserting your own words and pictures

- Add visual themes with a choice of foreground and background colours, and various styles of letters.

The Web Page Wizard is started after clicking **File** and **New...** from the Word Menu Bar. Then select **General Templates...** and click the **Web Pages** tab shown below.

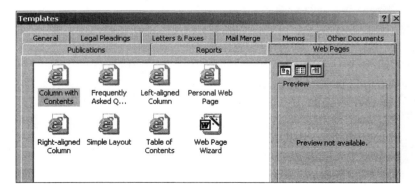

Click the **Web Page Wizard** icon shown on the previous page and you are presented with a welcome screen. Click **Next** and you are asked to enter a title for the new Web site. When the site is viewed in a Web browser, the title will appear on top of the Web page and in the title bar. You are also asked for the location (i.e. folder) where the pages will be saved on your hard disc. (Creating a folder for your Web site was discussed earlier). You can use the **Browse...** button shown below to search for the required folder.

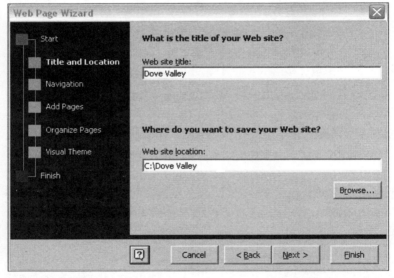

On clicking **Next** a choice of navigation frames appears, as shown on the next page. The navigation is a horizontal or vertical frame; inside this frame are clickable links to and from all of the Web pages on the site. The links are created automatically, based on the names you give to your Web pages, as described shortly. The layout of all of the pages is the same; each page displays the navigation frame and a frame which displays the contents of the selected page.

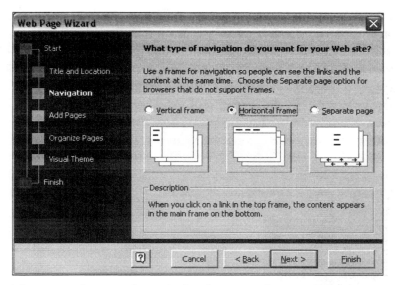

After you have selected the layout of your Web pages including frames and navigation as shown above, clicking **Next** launches the **Add pages to your site** box.

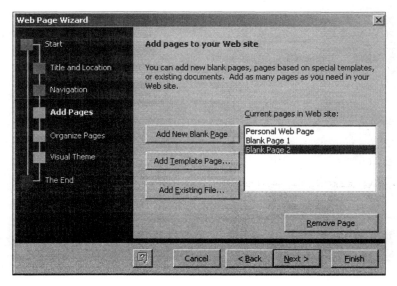

The **Add pages to your site** box shown on the previous page also allows you to remove pages and add a template page. Selecting **Add Template Page...** presents a choice of ready-made Web pages such as the page below, named **Left-aligned column**. Eventually all of the text and pictures provided in the template will be replaced by your own words and pictures for the Web site.

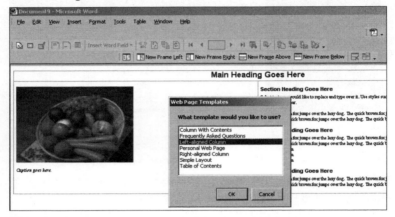

After clicking **OK**, a dialogue box appears allowing you to change the position of the links in the navigation frame and **Rename** them with your own names instead of **Blank Page 1**, **Blank Page 2**, etc.

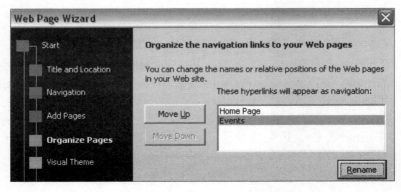

Click **Next** and you are given the chance to choose a visual theme; alternatively you can have a plain white background for your Web pages. If you click the **Add a visual theme** radio button and then click **Browse Themes...**, the **Theme** window opens as shown below, with a huge choice of named themes down the left-hand side.

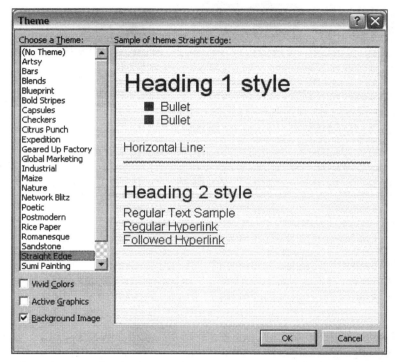

The themes include a choice of text styles, sizes and colours with various page background colours and patterns. There are also different styles for headings, bullets, horizontal lines, hyperlinks and links that have been followed, i.e. clicked. After you click **OK** a window appears telling you to click **Finish** to view the site.

After clicking **Finish,** the new site opens up as shown below. None of your own content has yet been entered but the basic page structure and navigation is in place.

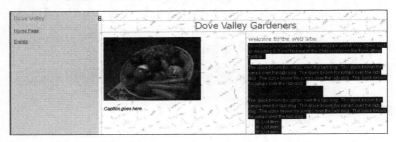

The screen extract above shows the navigation panel on the left-hand side. The text for the clickable links is underlined and based on the names given to the Web pages during the Web Wizard. In this example, the Web pages are called **Home Page** and **Events** and the Web site is called **Dove Valley.**

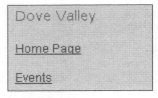

To replace the default text with your own, select the text then start typing your own words. To insert your own picture click over the default picture and press **Delete** to remove it. Then click **Insert, Picture** and **From File...** and browse to the folder containing your picture. Click **Insert** to place your picture on the page and if necessary drag one of the corner squares to adjust its size.

When all of the Web pages have been "customized" to include your own content they should be previewed in a Web browser as discussed on page 71, then edited if necessary and saved. Finally the pages are uploaded to a Web host as described earlier in this chapter and in the chapter **Publishing Your Web Site on the Internet.**

Getting Started with Serif WebPlus

Introduction

The next few chapters are based on Serif WebPlus, a very popular program for creating Web sites, available from Serif (Europe) Ltd at **www.serif.com**.

WebPlus is particularly suitable for home and small business users because:

- It's very easy to use and yet contains lots of powerful features, enabling you to create professional-looking Web sites from start to finish.

- Ready-made templates consisting of complete Web sites are provided; these can be customized with your own text, etc., to make your own Web site.

- The WebPlus package contains a useful manual, good help facilities, Web site design tips and ready-made artwork for inserting into your Web pages.

- The latest version of WebPlus is reasonably priced at around £60.

- You can get a fully working earlier version of WebPlus *completely free* by downloading it from **www.freeserifsoftware.com**. This will allow you to follow much of the work in this book, create a complete Web site and publish it on the Internet.

Launching WebPlus

WebPlus can be launched by clicking **Start**, **All Programs** and **Serif WebPlus**. Alternatively, double-click the **WebPlus** icon on the Windows Desktop. The program begins by displaying the **Startup Wizard** shown below.

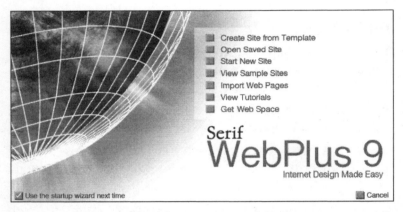

You can see from the above screen that there are several ways to start using the WebPlus program. For example, **Create Site from Template** allows you to take a ready-made Web site and tailor it to your own requirements. This means deleting the default text and pictures provided by WebPlus and replacing them with your own material, while maintaining the design features of the original template.

Even if you want to create your own Web site from scratch using a "blank canvas" approach, it's not a bad idea to have a look at some of the templates. By moving the cursor about a Web site template and clicking the various screen objects you'll soon get the feel of WebPlus and familiarize yourself with the main features of the software.

The option **Open Saved Site** on the **Startup Wizard** shown on the previous page allows you to continue developing a Web site that you have created and saved earlier. (Remember that while you are creating and developing a Web site, it is usually saved on the *local* hard disc inside of your own computer. Only when it is finished will the site be *uploaded* to the Internet and saved on a Web server computer for the whole world to see).

Start New Site in the **Startup Wizard** shown on the previous page presents the user with a blank Web page. Here you can set up your Web site structure and start entering text and pictures and even video and sound clips. This is quite easy in WebPlus and is discussed in more detail shortly.

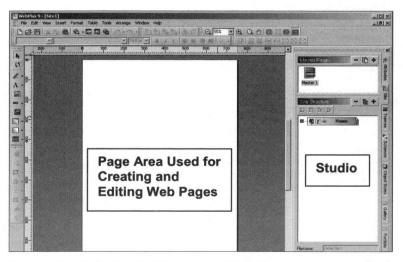

Down the right-hand side of the WebPlus screen are some panels with a series of clickable *tabs* down the extreme right. The panels and tabs are known as the WebPlus **Studio** and play a major role in creating, editing and organizing Web sites.

The **View Sample Sites** option listed on the **Startup Wizard** shown previously presents some stylish and professional-looking examples of Web sites created in WebPlus.

The **View Tutorials** option on the **Startup Wizard** leads to some very comprehensive notes on WebPlus. The notes present detailed descriptions of all of the main features in the program, created in the style of illustrated Web pages with links to various sub-sections, as shown below. The **Tutorials** in WebPlus are very clearly written and illustrated and are a good way to learn the more advanced features of the software.

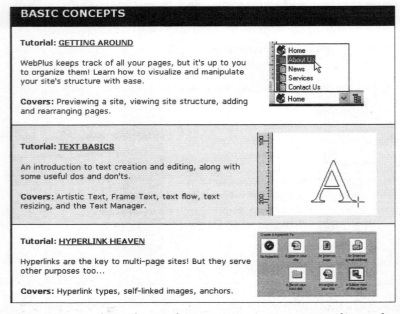

The next section shows how you can use a ready-made WebPlus template to create your own Web site. You simply insert your own text and graphics to replace the original material in the template.

The WebPlus Template Approach

First load up WebPlus so that the **Startup Wizard** appears, as shown on the previous page. Now select **Create Site from Template**. The following window appears, displaying thumbnail, i.e. miniature, pictures for the various templates, arranged in categories, such as **Business** and **Club**, etc., as shown below.

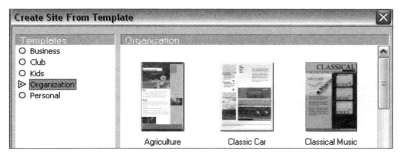

In this example, the **Classical Music** template was chosen from the **Organization** category. Click the required template and then click **Finish**. The **Classical Music** Web site opens up, displaying the Home Page.

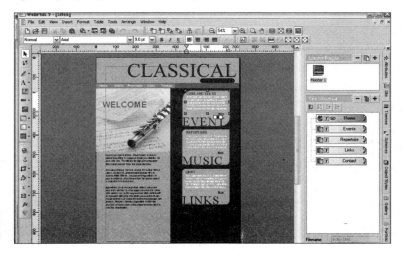

The Home Page on any Web site is usually the first one visitors see when browsing the Internet; typically the Home Page welcomes visitors, lists the contents of the other Web pages and provides "clickable" links between pages – often in the form of a *navigation bar*, as discussed shortly.

As shown on the previous page, the WebPlus screen displays, in the main page area, the Web page which is currently open for entering and editing text, pictures, etc. Across the top of the WebPlus screen is the Menu Bar and various toolbars, including the **Text** toolbar for formatting paragraphs and selecting different fonts, i.e. styles of lettering, as shown below.

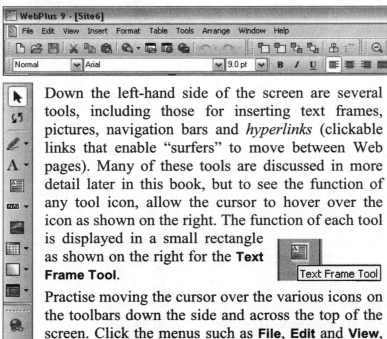

Down the left-hand side of the screen are several tools, including those for inserting text frames, pictures, navigation bars and *hyperlinks* (clickable links that enable "surfers" to move between Web pages). Many of these tools are discussed in more detail later in this book, but to see the function of any tool icon, allow the cursor to hover over the icon as shown on the right. The function of each tool is displayed in a small rectangle as shown on the right for the **Text Frame Tool**.

Practise moving the cursor over the various icons on the toolbars down the side and across the top of the screen. Click the menus such as **File**, **Edit** and **View**, etc., and have a look at the various menu options.

Entering Your Own Text into a Template

Move the cursor to the main page area and click over a paragraph; you will see that the text is contained in frames. When a frame is selected ready for editing, it displays eight small squares around its  perimeter. You can move the cursor to the required position and start altering the text, just like text in a word processor. Delete the text provided in the template and replace it with your own. You can also move the cursor to an outside edge of the frame (until it changes to a cross with four arrows) and then drag the frame to a new position.

Replacing a Template Picture with Your Own

WebPlus makes it very easy to replace an existing picture in a Web site template. Click the picture to select it, so that eight small squares appear around its perimeter. A small picture toolbar appears as shown below.

Now click the **Replace Picture** icon shown on the left and on the right above. The **Import Picture** dialogue box opens, allowing you to select a new picture from your hard disc. When you click the **Open** button, the new picture replaces the old one in the same size and position in the Web page.

Please note that inserting your own picture from scratch is covered in detail later in this book. Please also note that the picture toolbar above also contains tools for altering the brightness, contrast, colours and size of a picture.

The WebPlus Studio

Down the right-hand side of WebPlus you should see a large panel, known as the **Studio**. Down the extreme right of the **Studio** are various tabs; try clicking these and notice how the contents of the **Studio** panel change.

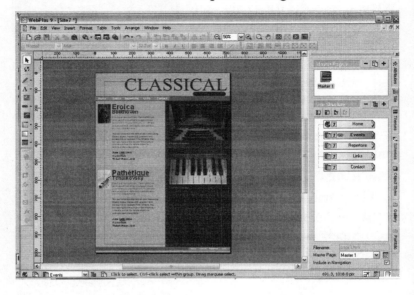

The **Site** tab shown above is one of the most important; it allows you to organize your Web site as a collection of individual linked Web pages. The Web pages are listed under **Site Structure**, shown enlarged on the right. Try double-clicking any of the entries such as **Events** or

Repertoire and notice what happens in the main page area.

As you double-click each of the entries in the **Studio** under **Site Structure**, notice also what happens in the Page Locator at the bottom left-hand corner of the WebPlus page. Click the down arrow on the right of the Page Locator and a menu pops up 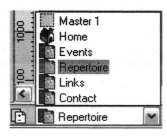 listing all of the pages in the Web site, as shown on the right above. Clicking a page name in the Page Locator is a quick way to move between the pages of a Web site while they are being created or edited. It's an alternative to double-clicking the page name in the **Site** panel.

Now try double-clicking the entry **Master 1** in the **Studio** panel or giving it a single-click in the **Page Locator** as shown above. The main page area now displays just a small amount of material as shown in the extract below.

Notice that the material shown above in the master page also appears on every other Web page on this sample Web site. The master page acts as a background *layer* for some or all of the Web pages. Master pages are created and edited in a similar way to the actual Web pages.

To create or edit a master page, make sure it is selected by double-clicking its icon in the **Master Pages** panel as shown on the right.

The Navigation Bar

Across every Web page on the **Classical Music** Web site is a bar as shown below.

Home	Events	Repertoire	Links	Contact

This is known as a *navigation bar* and each of the words **Home, Events, Repertoire**, etc., is a clickable link to the named Web page. When you create a Web site consisting of a number of Web pages, it's a simple matter to insert a navigation bar, as discussed later. The navigation bar is created as part of a master page and therefore appears on some or all of the individual Web pages. (A master page can be applied to every Web page or just to selected pages.)

The navigation bar is automatically based on the names of the pages in the **Site Structure**, as shown on the right for the **Classical Music** Web site template. The **1** against each entry in the list of page names shown on the right indicates that all of these Web pages are based on the master

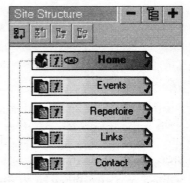

page **Master 1**. The small icon representing an eye, shown against **Home** above, indicates that the Home Page is currently open for editing in the main page area of WebPlus.

Colour Schemes

The **Schemes** tab on the far right of the WebPlus screen is particularly useful for customizing the colour scheme of a Web site template (or any other completed Web site).

There are many different colour schemes to choose from;

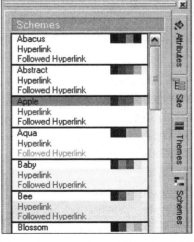

these change the colour of the text, the background colours and the colours in ready-made objects such as banners and logos. To apply a new scheme, select its name, such as **Apple**, from the **Schemes** panel on the right of the screen.

There are many other features accessed through the tabs on the right-hand side of the screen, which can be used to add features, alter the appearance of a completed Web site or customize a template. Some of the main features available from the **Studio** tabs are discussed in more detail shortly.

Previewing a Web Site

It's important to see what a Web site looks like in a Web browser such as Internet Explorer; this is how visitors to the site will see it. WebPlus can detect browsers installed on your computer and use them to preview the Web site.

You can try this by previewing one of the template Web sites which WebPlus provides, such as the **Classical Music** template discussed earlier. With the Web site displayed in the main page area of WebPlus, click the **Preview** icon on the toolbar across the top of the screen. Then select **Preview Site in Internet Explorer 6.00** (or whatever browser you are using) from the menu which appears. The browser opens displaying the Home Page of the template Web site. Click each button on the navigation bar to move between all of the Web pages and check their appearance.

Close the Web browser and return to WebPlus to edit the pages and make any changes arising from the preview.

Setting Up Your Own Web Site

Planning and Preparation

Before starting to create the actual Web pages, it's a good idea to give some thought to the content of each page. In this example I have decided to create a simple Web site to help anyone visiting Rome for the first time. Obviously for the purposes of this book, the Web site will be kept very simple and will only extend to three pages. However, this should be enough to demonstrate the creation of Web pages containing text and pictures; the pages will also include clickable links to Web pages on the same site. There may also be links to Web pages on other Web sites stored on other computers.

The Rome Web site will consist of a Home Page welcoming visitors and describing the contents of the site. A second page will list some of the main sights to see in Rome and a third page will give help on getting around the city.

Once the planning and preparation have been completed it is a relatively simple matter to enter the text and pictures into one of the many programs available for creating the Web pages.

The main stages in the planning and preparation of a simple Web site are as follows:

- Using pencil and paper, draw a plan showing the main pages with links, pictures and a rough idea of the text.

- Locate the required photographs either as images on your hard disc or as photographic prints. Prints will have to be scanned and saved on the hard disc.

- Create a new folder and store in it those photographs needed for the Web site.

- Large photographs cause Web pages to load slowly, causing frustration to visitors to your site. Use the methods discussed in the chapter **Working with Photographs** later in this book to reduce the size of photographs saved as files on your hard disc.

The Sketch Plan

Although you can create your Web site by typing it straight into the Web creation software, a rough plan will enable you to decide what pages are required and any photographs which need to be located or obtained.

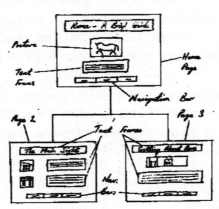

Organizing Your Pictures

Any pictures, photos, etc., required for your Web site, should be organized in their own separate folder to make them easy to locate quickly. The Rome Web site will include four photographs taken with a digital camera and stored in a folder called **Selected Rome Photos**, as shown below.

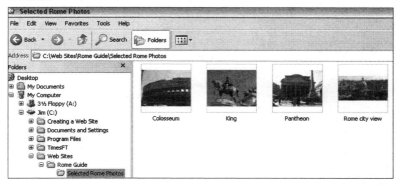

The location on the hard disc of the folder containing the photos (shown in the **Address** bar above) is:

C:\Web Sites\Rome Guide\Selected Rome Photos

C: refers to the computer's hard disc and **Web Sites, Rome Guide** and **Selected Rome Photos** are folders which have been specially created in the Windows Explorer. This hierarchy of folders can be seen in the left-hand panel of the above screenshot and is shown enlarged below.

Setting Up the Page Structure in WebPlus

The Home Page is normally the first page you see when you enter a Web site. Its purpose is to welcome visitors to the site, outline the contents of the site and provide clickable links to the other pages. To create a new Web page from a blank page, select **Start New Site** from the WebPlus **Startup Wizard** shown in the last chapter. The following screen appears.

As shown above, the blank page is ready for you to start entering text and pictures, etc. This is discussed shortly.

WebPlus makes it very easy to organize the structure of your Web site, i.e. the arrangement of the pages and the way they are connected. The **Site Structure** is shown in the right-hand panel above, currently only displaying the **Home Page**. The right-hand panel in WebPlus is known as the **Studio** and is shown enlarged on the next page.

The **Studio** panel is a very useful feature in WebPlus; it allows you to insert and remove Web pages from your site and to control the appearance of pages using different colours, styles and ready-made artwork. Down the right-hand side of the

Studio are several tabs which display different panels enabling you to alter various aspects of the Web site, discussed later. For now we will concentrate on the **Site** tab shown above, since this controls the structure of the site.

When you start a new site, the **Site Structure** contains just one entry, **Home**, representing the Home Page, as shown above. Anything you type or insert on the main blank page shown on the left on the previous page will become the Home Page of your new Web site.

The rough sketch plan for the Rome site determined that we will have a second page called **The Main Sights** and another called **Getting About Rome**. We can insert a new Web page by clicking the + sign to the right of **Site Structure** shown above and below. Doing this twice results in two new pages as shown below. (To remove a Web page, you click the entry for the page to highlight it and then click the − sign as shown on the right.)

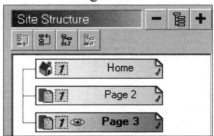

Please note that the main page area of the screen displays the page whose entry is currently highlighted in the **Studio** as shown at the bottom of the previous page. To display a different page in the main page area, double-click its entry in the **Studio**. The page which is currently being displayed in the page area is denoted by an eye icon in its entry in the **Studio**, as shown on the right.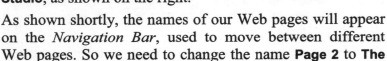

As shown shortly, the names of our Web pages will appear on the *Navigation Bar*, used to move between different Web pages. So we need to change the name **Page 2** to **The Main Sights** and **Page 3** to **Getting About Rome**.

This is done by right-clicking over the page entry in the **Studio** panel. A small menu pops up from which you select **Page Properties...**. This opens the dialogue box shown below in which you enter the new name in the **Page name** bar. **The Main Sights** replaces **Page 2** and **Getting About Rome** replaces **Page 3**.

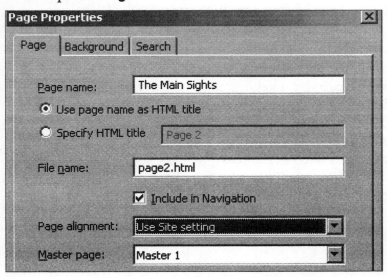

The renamed pages are shown in the extract from the WebPlus **Studio** shown below. Although there is insufficient room to display the names in full on the entries in the **Studio**, they will appear in full on the navigation bar, as discussed shortly.

We have now set up a simple structure for the Rome Web site, consisting of a Home Page and two additional pages. These are ready to start entering the text and graphics as discussed shortly. However, we have first to consider how the pages will be linked so that the user can move easily between pages.

Master Pages

WebPlus uses *Master Pages* to add features which will appear on some or all of the pages of a Web site. This is similar to pre-printed stationery or headed notepaper. All Web pages therefore comprise two *layers*; a background layer consisting of the master page and a foreground layer containing the text and pictures of individual Web pages.

The idea is that you set up a master page containing certain features which are to be repeated throughout the Web site. Then you specify which of your Web pages the master page is to apply to. You can have more than one master page and apply them to different Web pages. Shortly we will create a master page, **Master 1**, and insert on it a *navigation bar* to allow the user to move around the site. Master pages can be managed using the **Studio** in a similar way to the ordinary Web pages, as shown below.

Double-click the icon for **Master 1** as shown above and a new blank master page appears in the main page area.

Notice that an eye icon appears on the **Master 1** icon, showing that **Master 1** is the page currently being created or edited in the main page area of WebPlus. Although the features from the master page may appear on every Web page, you can only edit them on the master page, not on an ordinary Web page. To edit a master page, double-

click the master page icon in the **Studio**, so that the eye appears as shown above. The master page will now appear in the main page area ready for creating or editing.

In the above extract, the − and + signs allow you to insert or delete master pages and the icon in between enables you to manage your master pages.

The number of the master page used by a Web page is shown in the entry for the Web page in the **Studio**, as shown on the right. In this example, all of the Web pages use **Master 1**.

To change the page which is being created or edited in the main page area, double-click the page entry in the **Studio**. Alternatively select from the Page Locator menu which appears just above the **Start** menu at the bottom left of the WebPlus screen, as shown below. Several other useful icons appear next to the Page Locator; to see their function allow the cursor to hover over them.

Creating a Navigation Bar

The navigation bar displays clickable buttons to allow you to move between pages on your Web site as shown below.

Home The Main Sights Getting About Rome

WebPlus makes the creation of navigation bars very easy by allowing you to select from a range of ready-made bars in various styles. WebPlus automatically fills in the names on the buttons, based on the page names you have provided in the WebPlus **Studio**, as discussed previously. For example, in the above example, my three Web pages were **Home, The Main Sights** and **Getting About Rome**.

First, we make sure that the main page area is showing **Master 1** (initially blank), denoted by an eye in the entry in the **Studio** or by the name **Master 1** appearing in the **Page Locator** at the bottom of the screen, as shown on the previous page.

Next, from the right-hand side of the WebPlus screen, select the **Themes** tab. Now select **View Types from Theme Graphics** and start scrolling down this panel. You can see that the **Theme Graphics** contain lots of ready-made features including banners and buttons. (Many of these contain "dummy" text which can be deleted and replaced with your own words). In the **Categories** panel under **Types** you will see **Horizontal Navbar** and further down the list **Vertical Navbar**. Either of these can be used to provide a navigation bar for the Rome Web site.

Navigation bars and Theme Graphics can also be inserted after clicking the **Insert Navigation Bar** icon on the toolbar on the left of the WebPlus screen.

You could, if you prefer, choose a vertical navigation bar as shown in the example on the right.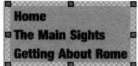

Choosing **Horizontal Navbar** presents a choice of horizontal navigation bars in many different styles, as shown in the small extract below.

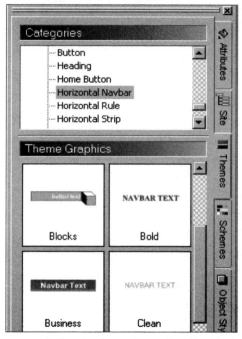

Now choose one of the designs for a horizontal navigation bar as shown in the small extract above and drag its icon and drop it on the main page area of **Master 1**. (Dragging means clicking and holding down the left mouse button then moving the selected object to its new location before releasing the mouse button to drop the object).

The navigation bar appears on the page area of **Master 1**.

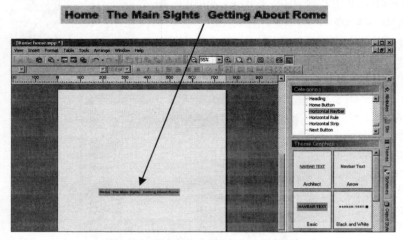

Now the navigation bar can be highlighted in the page area by clicking (so that 8 small squares appear). Then the navigation bar can be moved around the page by dragging. You will probably need to adjust the position of the bar on **Master 1**, after you have started entering the text and graphics on the main Web pages, as discussed shortly.

Please also note that you can edit the navigation bar by right-clicking anywhere over the bar while the **Master 1** page is displayed in the main page area. Then select **Edit Navigation Bar**.... One of the options on the resulting *context menu* is to switch on or off **Make all buttons the same size**. Switching this off adjusts the size of the buttons to suit the button text as shown in the navigation bar above.

Summary – Web Site Structure

So now we have set up the basic structure for the simple Rome Web site. At this stage there are three Web pages including the Home Page and two others. These are blank except for the navigation bar which appears on every page.

The navigation bar was created on a master page – **Master 1**. Any items you create on a master page appear on all of the Web pages to which you have applied that master page. You can have more than one master page and apply them to different Web pages. For example, we could base the **Home Page** and **Getting About Rome** on **Master 1** and base **The Main Sights** on a new master page, such as **Master 2**, for example. This structure would appear in the WebPlus **Studio** as shown below.

Context-Sensitive Menus

Many tasks in WebPlus (and Windows programs in general) can be accomplished after *right-clicking* over an object on the screen. This launches a *context menu*, with a set of options of particular relevance to the selected object.

So far we have seen how to set up the *structure* of a simple Web site consisting of three pages. At this stage the Web site is just an empty shell containing no text or pictures. We have created a master page, **Master 1**, containing a navigation bar as shown on the right. When the Web site is displayed in a Web browser such as Internet Explorer, the master page will not appear as a separate entity. Instead it will be present as a background *layer* in every Web page we have applied it to, as discussed in the last

Master 1

chapter. In the Rome Web site used in this example, **Master 1** only contains the navigation bar used to move between pages on the Web site, as shown below.

Home    **The Main Sights**    **Getting About Rome**

The navigation bar provides clickable links allowing you to move between pages on the site. In this example the navigation bar will appear on every Web page.

Home The Main Sights Getting About Rome

We may need to adjust the position of the navigation bar on the page to suit the finished text and graphics. Any changes to the navigation bar must be made by editing the master page, **Master 1**, not the individual Web pages.

So now we have to start entering text and pictures to arrive at the finished Rome Web pages, which will appear in a Web browser as shown below.

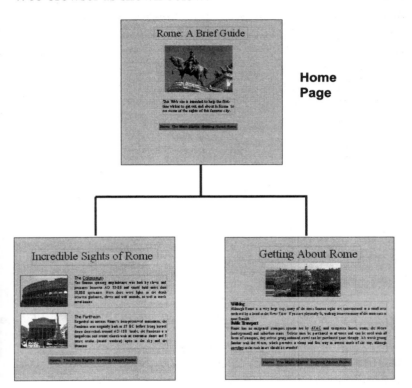

Entering Text in WebPlus

There are two main ways of entering text in WebPlus; *artistic* text and text entered into a *text frame*. For the time being we will only consider text entered into a frame. This is just like entering text into a word processor. In fact if you are entering a large amount of text, you can switch between WebPlus and a built-in word processor called WritePlus, to take advantage of facilities such as a spelling checker and word count. Then switch back to WebPlus with your new text already inserted into the text frame.

Selecting the Home Page

Select the (empty) Home Page by clicking the **Site** tab in WebPlus. Now *double-click* the **Home** entry, under **Site Structure** in the WebPlus **Studio** as shown on the right. The page name **Home** should 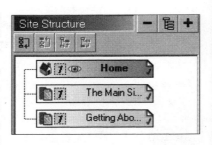 now appear in the **Page Locator** at the bottom left-hand corner of the screen, as shown below.

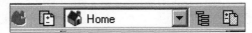

This shows that the **Home** page is open for entering and editing text and pictures in the main page area of WebPlus. This is also confirmed by the small eye icon to the left of **Home** in the **Site Structure** panel above. At this stage the **Home** page is blank except for the navigation bar, as discussed earlier.

Entering the Text for the Home Page

Now select the **Text Frame Tool**, shown on the right, from the toolbar down the left-hand side of the WebPlus screen. Move the cursor (now in the 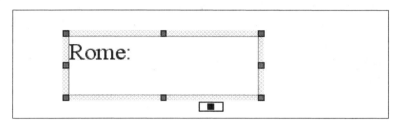 shape of a cross) onto the page area where it can be dragged to create a rectangle of the required size.

The eight "handles" around the perimeter of a selected text frame can be dragged to make further adjustments to the frame size. A flashing cursor appears in the frame ready for you to begin typing. When a text frame is selected, the WebPlus screen displays a set of text formatting tools along the top, just like a word processor, as shown below.

As in a word processor, you can apply effects such as bold, italics, centering within the frame, etc. The effects can be applied before you begin typing. Alternatively, after entering the text, highlight it by dragging the cursor over it and then select the required effect.

The small rectangle shown below a selected frame indicates that all of the text contained in the frame is simultaneously visible on the screen. Other symbols indicate text overflowing a frame and also text spanning two or more *linked* frames.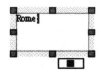

Moving a Text Frame

One of the advantages of placing your words in a text frame is that the frame and its contents can easily be moved around the page. Click anywhere inside the frame to select it, so that the eight small squares appear. Hover the cursor over one of the sides of the frame until a cross with four arrow heads appears. Now, keeping the left mouse button held down, drag the text frame to your chosen position on the WebPlus page.

Using the WritePlus Word Processor

For longer pieces of text, WebPlus has a built-in word processor, known as WritePlus. You can move straight from a text frame in WebPlus into the WritePlus word processor. When you have finished using the word processor it's a simple matter to move back to the WebPlus page with the word processed text already inserted.

For example, to insert the main paragraph on the Rome Home Page, insert a text frame of the required size, as described earlier. Start the WritePlus word processor by selecting **Edit** and **Edit Story**. WritePlus opens in its own window ready for you to start entering text.

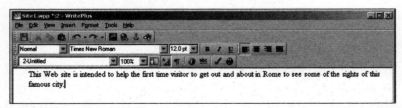

When you have finished entering text into the WritePlus word processor, click **File** and **Close** to return to the main WebPlus screen.

You are returned to the WebPlus screen with the text from the word processor already inserted in the WebPlus text frame, as shown below.

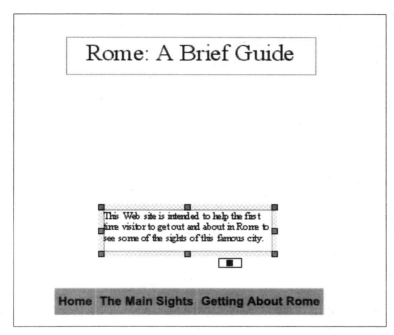

The text for this simple Web page is now complete. You can change the text in the boxes at any time, for example to select bold, italics, etc., or to change the font size.

Adjusting a Master Page Element

To adjust the position of the navigation bar (or edit any other elements in a background layer provided by a master page), you must select the master page for editing. Double-click the **Master** entry at the top of the WebPlus **Studio**; the small eye icon should now be visible next to the **Master** icon as shown on the right.

Working With Pictures

As mentioned earlier in this book, you need to know where to find any pictures or photos stored on your hard disc. If possible the images required for your Web pages should be organized into a separate folder. The photos for the Rome Web site are shown below in the Windows Explorer.

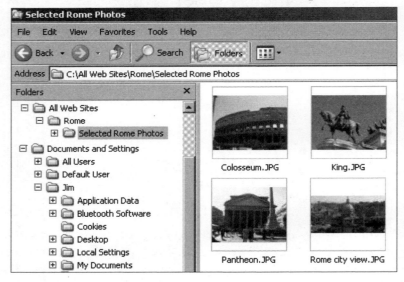

Photographs for use in Web pages are often saved in the JPEG format, with the JPG file name extension, for example **King.JPG**, as shown above. The GIF format is also a popular format for Web images. These file types are discussed in more detail in Chapter 9.

When you insert a picture into a Web page in WebPlus (or any other program), you will have to provide the exact location (on your hard disc) of the folder containing the photo. In this example, the location (or *path*) is:

C:\All Web Sites\Rome\Selected Rome Photos

Inserting a Picture into WebPlus

From the toolbar down the left-hand side of the WebPlus screen, select the **Import Picture** icon shown on the right. This opens up the **Import Picture** dialogue box shown below.

You need to click the down arrow to the right of the **Look in** bar shown above. This will enable you to locate, on your hard disc, the folder which contains the required image. To make sure you have found the right image make sure the **Preview** checkbox is ticked so that a thumbnail of the image is displayed, as shown above. Click the required file name, **King.JPG**, in the example above, so that it appears in the **File name** bar at the bottom of the dialogue box.

Now click **Open** to start placing the image on the WebPlus page; as shown on the next page, this couldn't be easier.

Now when the cursor is moved over the main page
area in WebPlus, it changes to a cross and a small
rectangle. Use the left-hand button of the mouse to
drag the picture to the required size. When you release the
mouse button, the picture appears selected, i.e. with eight
small squares around its perimeter, as shown below. You
can now fine tune the size of the picture using one of the
corner handles. While the eight squares are visible the
picture can be moved into its final position by dragging
with the left mouse button held down.

Rome: A Brief Guide

This Web site is intended to help the first-time
visitor to get out and about in Rome to see
some of the sights of this famous city.

Home   The Main Sights   Getting Around Rome

Saving a Web Site on Your Hard Disc

At this stage we have created the Home Page of a Web site by entering text in frames and also inserting a picture. It is normal for each of the pages in a Web site to have an individual file name; it is also normal for the Home Page to be given the special name, **index.html**. This can be seen by clicking **Edit** and **Page Properties...** in WebPlus with **Home** selected in the **Site** panel. The **Page Properties** dialogue box opens showing the **File name** as **index.html**.

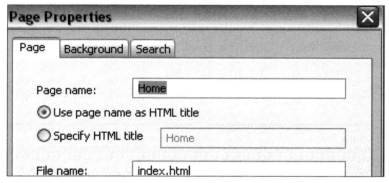

Please note that the **Page name** shown above is the name which appears in the **Studio** of WebPlus in the **Site** panel. When a page is viewed in a Web browser, such as Internet Explorer, it is the **File name**, such as **index.html**, which appears in the address bar, as shown below.

Both the **Page name** and the **File name** can be edited in the **Page Properties** dialogue box shown above.

Although the Home Page should remain as **index.html**, the other pages of your Web site can be renamed in the **Page Properties** dialogue box, by replacing the default file names **page2.html** and **page3.html**, etc.

As discussed earlier, the file names of individual Web pages are used by the Web browser and displayed in the browser's address bar. However, you do not save individual Web pages in WebPlus; instead the complete Web site is saved as a WebPlus document or *project file*.

The Rome site only consists of a Home Page and two more almost blank pages, but it's still a good idea to save the site at regular intervals as the work progresses. Click **File** and **Save** or **Save As...** to open the **Save As** dialogue box.

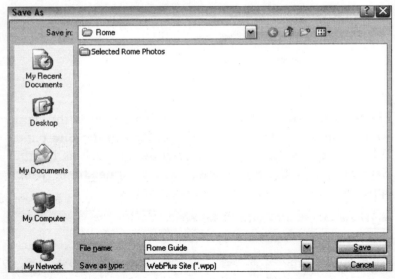

From the drop-down list next to **Save in** shown above, select the folder in which you wish to save your new Web site. The folder **Rome** is used in this example.

Now enter a name for the site next to **File name**, such as **Rome Guide**, for example. Notice at the bottom of the **Save As** dialogue box that the complete multi-page Web site is being saved as a **WebPlus Site** with the .wpp file name extension, as shown below next to **Save as type**.

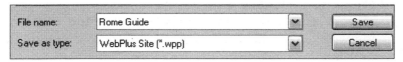

Click the **Save** button shown above and the site will be saved in the folder of your choice, as shown in the Windows Explorer below.

You can see above that the Web site, **Rome Guide** is saved as a **WebPlus Document** in the folder **Rome**, having the path **C:\All Web Sites\Rome**. Also in the **Rome** folder shown above is a subfolder called **Selected Rome Photos**, containing the four images necessary for the Web site.

Save and **Save As**

Select **File** and **Save** or click the disc icon on the Standard Toolbar to continue saving the Web site with the same file name and folder. Use **File** and **Save As...** if you want to change the Web site name or the folder location used to save the site.

Completing the Rome Web Site

At this stage the part-finished Rome Web site is saved on the hard disc of the local computer. When the site is finally completed it will be copied or *uploaded* to the Internet and saved on a Web server. For the time being the developing Web site will continue to be saved on the local hard disc. Earlier in this chapter, the methods of entering text and pictures were described. These methods can now be used to complete the remaining two pages of the Rome Web site.

To start work on the second page, **The Main Sights**, double-click its entry in the WebPlus **Studio,** as shown on the right. The small eye icon should appear against the entry for the page. The page name should 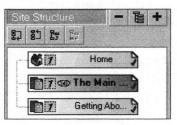 also be displayed in the Page Locator at the bottom left of the screen, as shown below.

The second page, **The Main Sights**, is now displayed in the main page area of WebPlus, ready for text and pictures to be entered as described earlier for the Home Page. A page completed earlier would be opened for editing in the main page area in the same way.

The above procedure is then repeated to complete the third page, **Getting About Rome**.

At this point the first draft of the simple Rome Web site is now complete and will appear in a Web browser (such as Internet Explorer) as shown at the beginning of this chapter. It should now be saved again as described earlier.

7

Finishing Off Your Web Site

Previous chapters have shown how text, pictures and a navigation bar can be added to a Web page, using Serif WebPlus. This chapter describes the insertion of extra features such as additional links or hyperlinks connecting Web pages, as well as artistic effects and sound and video clips. Also discussed is the previewing of a site in a Web browser and final editing prior to uploading to the Internet.

Hyperlinks

A *hyperlink* or *link* is a clickable screen object (such as a piece of text or a picture) which enables the visitor to a Web site to move to another page. A text hyperlink is displayed underlined and may be in a different colour from other text. When you pass the cursor over a hyperlink, the cursor changes to a hand. A hyperlink can be used, for example, to:

- Open up another Web page in your browser. This may be on your own Web site or on another Web site anywhere on the World Wide Web.

- Display a full-sized version of a picture after a thumbnail or miniature version is clicked.

- Clicking a link such as **Send Us An E-mail** causes a visitor's e-mail program to open up with the Web site owner's e-mail address already inserted.

Inserting a Text Hyperlink

Enter a suitable piece of text for the link. In this example I will create on the Home Page **Rome: a Brief Guide** another link to the page **Getting About Rome**. (We already have such a link on the navigation bar, but this hyperlink will serve as a convenient example). This text is typed into a text frame onto the required Web page. Now select (by dragging with the mouse) the text for the link, as shown on  the left. Right-click over the highlighted text and select **Hyperlink...** from the menu which appears. Alternatively click the **Hyperlink** icon (shown right) on the toolbar down the left-hand side of the screen. The **Hyperlinks** window opens as shown below, presenting several possible destinations to which you can create a hyperlink.

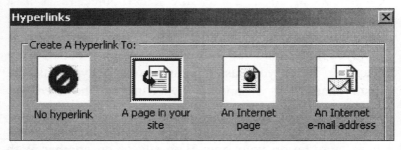

In the above example, a link to **A page in your site** has been selected and the required page **Getting About Rome** has been chosen from the drop-down menu next to **Page name:**.

When you click **OK** as shown on the previous page, you are returned to the WebPlus editing screen, with the text for the hyperlink underlined. The colour of the text in the hyperlink is determined by the colour scheme selected in the WebPlus **Studio**, as discussed earlier in this book.

Getting About Rome

Testing a Hyperlink

To see if a hyperlink works, enter **File** and **Preview Site** and select your Web browser, such as Internet Explorer, from the menu which appears.

Preview Site	▶	Preview in Window
Publish Site	▶	Preview Page in Internet Explorer 6.00
Print...	Ctrl+P	✓ Preview Site in Internet Explorer 6.00

Your Web site opens in the Web browser. Click the new link and check that this opens up the destination Web page.

To create a hyperlink to another Web site somewhere on the Internet, select **An Internet page** from the **Hyperlinks** window shown on the previous page. Then enter the address of the new page at the bottom of the **Hyperlinks** window, such as:

An Internet page

http://www.jimsweb.co.uk/index.html

To invite visitors to your site to send e-mails, select **An Internet e-mail address** and enter your e-mail address in the **E-mail:** bar at the bottom of the **Hyperlinks** window. The link text might be something like "**E-mail Us**".

An Internet e-mail address

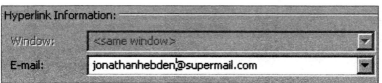

Hyperlink Information:	
Window:	<same window>
E-mail:	jonathanhebden@supermail.com

Using a Picture as a Hyperlink

A picture can be used as a hyperlink in a similar way to the text hyperlink discussed earlier, linking to another page on the same site or to a page on an entirely different Web site, perhaps in another part of the world.

Displaying a Full Size Picture

However, a common use for a picture link is to use it to display a full-size version of an image. Pictures are often displayed in a small size or as a thumbnail. This saves time when a page is first loaded; however, a visitor to a site might be interested to see the full-size version.

The Pantheon
Regarded as ancient Rome's best-preserved monument, the Pantheon was originally built in 27 BC before being burned down then rebuilt around AD 120. Its title, the Pantheon is a magnificent and ornate church with an enormous dome and 9 metre oculus (round window) open to the sky and the elements.

 First select the image so that eight small rectangles appear, as shown above. Now select the **Hyperlinks... option** from the menu window after right-clicking over the picture.

A fullsize view of this picture

Alternatively click **Hyperlinks** icon on the left-hand toolbar as before. Now select **A fullsize view of this picture** and click **OK**. You are returned to the WebPlus editing screen. Select the **Preview Site** option as described earlier and check the picture hyperlink in your Web browser. When you click the picture it should open up and fill most of the screen.

Inserting Special Effects

WebPlus is packed full of special effects and ready-made artwork to enable you to make your Web site more interesting; there are too many special features to mention here, but a few samples are given as a taster.

Artistic Text

The **Artist Text** tool on the toolbar on the left-hand side of the screen allows you to drag letters to any size you want. Simply click the tool and drag out, to the required size, the letter A which appears. Release the mouse button and begin typing the artistic text.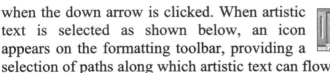

Artistic text can also be made to follow various paths, selected from the menu which flies out from the **Artistic Text** tool when the down arrow is clicked. When artistic text is selected as shown below, an icon appears on the formatting toolbar, providing a selection of paths along which artistic text can flow

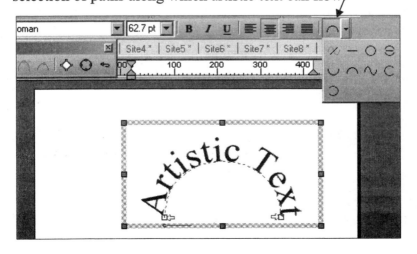

Banners and Buttons

If you experiment by clicking the tabs on the right-hand side of the WebPlus **Studio** you will find lots of ready-made artwork. For example, if you select the **Themes** tab and **Theme Graphics**, a huge range of banners and buttons, etc., is available. To use a graphic, drag it from the studio panel and drop it over the Web page in the main page area.

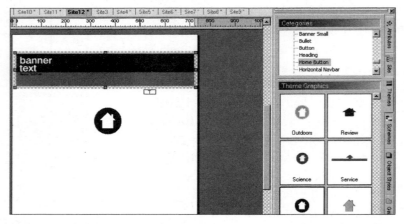

You can now drag the artwork to the required size. The colours and any text in a piece of artwork can be customized after double-clicking the object on the screen. To alter the wording or the font in a banner, for example, double-click the banner then enter the new text in the dialogue box which appears, as shown below.

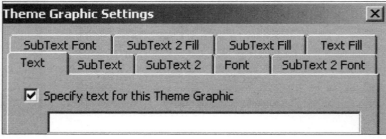

The **Gallery** tab presents a range of artwork including a number of buttons and arrows. For example, in the **Rollovers** panel under **Categories** and **Designs** there are buttons and arrows for **email, Home, Next** and **Back**, etc.

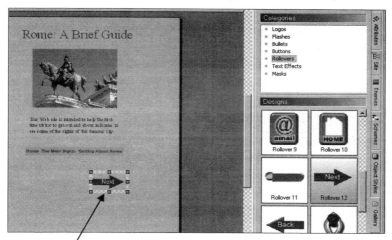

To use the **Next** arrow in a Web page, for example, drag and drop the arrow over the page. With the arrow still selected (with eight squares visible), double-click the arrow. This brings up the **Rollover Graphic** dialogue box. You can make the **Next** arrow into a hyperlink by clicking the **Set...** button then choosing a destination Web page, etc., from the **Hyperlinks** dialogue box which appears. This was discussed earlier in this chapter. Then the **Next** arrow can be used as a clickable hyperlink link to another Web page, another Web site or some other destination.

To help visitors move around your Web site, other buttons and arrows such as **Home, Back** and **email** can be made into "live" hyperlinks in a similar way.

Multimedia Objects

WebPlus makes it easy to incorporate multimedia objects such as sound and video clips into a Web page; you can also include animated pictures and "marquees" – moving text which scrolls across the screen. These multimedia inserts may not be necessary or appropriate for every Web site, depending on the context. However, your Web site may be intended to keep in touch with friends or family, perhaps in faraway places. Why not personalize the site with some simple animation and light-hearted sound and video clips, especially if younger children are involved. As shown on the next few pages, it's not at all difficult or technically challenging. However, it's a good idea to use multimedia objects sparingly as they do impose an additional burden on a Web site, making it slower to load and also using up Web storage space.

When visitors to your Web site try to play a sound or video clip, they will need to have compatible software installed on their computer, such as Apple QuickTime, and RealPlayer. Some of these players can be downloaded free from the Internet, while Microsoft Windows includes its own built-in Windows Media Player.

Inserting Multimedia

WebPlus provides a very large number of moving pictures known as *animated GIFs*. The word GIF refers to a popular file format used to save pictures containing few colours.

From the left-hand toolbar on WebPlus, select the **Insert Hotspot** icon shown on the right. A fly-out menu appears as shown below, with icons representing the various types of media.

Animated GIFs

The first icon on the left of the fly-out menu shown on the previous page allows you to insert a moving graphic. When you click the icon shown on the right, WebPlus will open the **Import Animated GIF** dialogue box, requiring you to select an image.

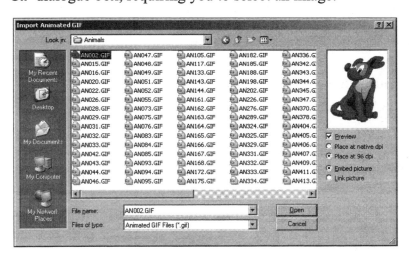

There are hundreds of animated GIFs and other artwork provided with WebPlus. Make sure you have installed the separate Resources CD which is provided as part of the package. If WebPlus does not automatically open the folders containing the animated GIFs, click the down arrow to the right of the **Look in:** bar and select the following folder containing the GIFs:

C:\Program Files\Serif\WebPlus\9.0\WebArtRes\Animated

There are lots of animated GIFs in various categories such as **Animals, Birds, Cartoons, People** and **Sport** for example.

When you click the **Open** button you are returned to the Web page, where you drag the cursor to insert the GIF at the size you require. Please note that the GIF is not animated when it is placed on the page in WebPlus. In order to see the GIF moving you need to preview the Web site in a Web  browser, such as Internet Explorer. This is done by selecting **File** and **Preview Site** or clicking the **HTML Preview** icon, as discussed elsewhere in this book.

Inserting an Animated Marquee

The animated marquee is a piece of text which scrolls across the screen. Click the icon shown on the left and below.

The **Animated Marquee Wizard** appears, allowing you to enter the text to be scrolled and to choose colours, font style and the direction and speed of scrolling.

Allowing Popups

To test the **Animated Marquee**, you will need to **Preview** the Web site, as discussed earlier. If your browser, such as Internet Explorer, has a feature to block items which "pop up" on the screen, you will need to temporarily unblock it. This may apply to multimedia screen objects such as animated marquees and sound and video clips, discussed shortly. On Internet Explorer, click the Information Bar at the top of the screen and then click **Allow Blocked Content....**

Allow Blocked Content...
What's the Risk?

Information Bar Help

Inserting Sound and Video Clips

A sound clip might be a voice message or a piece of music, for example. Click the **Insert Sound Clip** icon on the fly-out **Insert Hotspot** bar.

A **Sound Dialogue** box opens, allowing you to browse for the sound file on your hard disc, as shown below.

You can choose what sort of icon will be displayed on the Web page. This will be used to launch the sound clip when displayed in a Web browser. When you click **OK** you are returned to the Web page with the sound clip icon inserted. The icon can be dragged to a suitable size. In order to test the sound clip you will need to preview the site in a Web browser such as Internet Explorer, as discussed elsewhere.

Inserting a Video Clip

After clicking the **Insert Video Clip** icon as shown on the right, the method for inserting a video clip is very similar to that for a sound clip,

You will need to set your Web browser to allow popups before testing multimedia objects inserted into a Web page.

Previewing Your Web Site

Before uploading a site to a Web server computer on the Internet, it's important to see how the site will look in a Web browser such as Internet Explorer. The **Preview** option in WebPlus can be launched by clicking **File** and **Preview Site** as shown below. Alternatively click the down arrow to the right of the preview icon on the WebPlus toolbar. A menu of preview options opens as shown below.

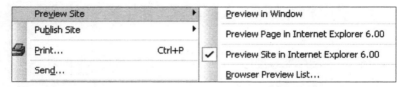

The list of options shown on the right above should include any Web browsers, such as Internet Explorer, installed on your computer. The names of any installed browsers can be checked by selecting **Browse Preview List...** above.

If you choose one of the options starting **Preview Page** or **Preview Site**, your Web browser will be launched, displaying the current page or site as it will appear to visitors to your Web site when it is installed on the Internet.

The **Preview Site** option will allow you to test the navigation bar and any other links, to move between all of the pages of your site. If you have inserted any animations or sound or video clips you will need to switch off any "popup" blocking features in your Web browser, before testing them. (Multimedia objects can only be tested in the **Preview** facility). Shown below is **The Main Sights** page of the Rome site, previewed in Internet Explorer.

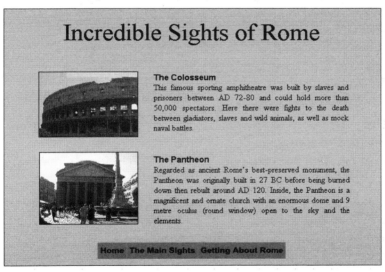

If you click the **Preview in Window** option on the **Preview** menu shown earlier, the Web pages are displayed in WebPlus rather than in your Web browser. The **Preview** toolbar, shown on the next page pops up allowing you to check the Web pages at various screen resolutions in *pixels*. A pixel (or picture element) is the smallest rectangle which can be displayed on the screen. For example, **1024 x 768** means the screen is made up of a grid of 1024 pixels horizontally and 768 pixels vertically.

The Home Page of the Rome site is shown below previewed in WebPlus after selecting **Preview in Window**.

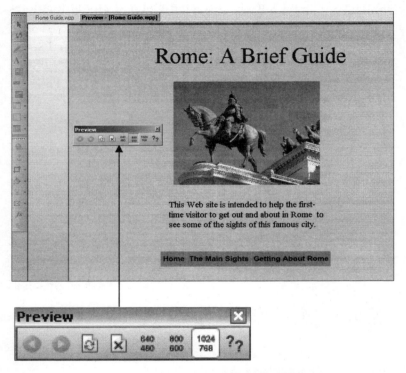

You can view the Web pages at three different screen resolutions by clicking each pair of pixels in turn, as shown above. To specify your own width and height in pixels, click the two question marks shown above, to open the **Preview Custom Size** dialogue shown on the right. Enter your own figures for **Width** and **Height**.

Editing Web Pages

After you have previewed a new Web site, you will probably want to make some changes; perhaps to use a different text font, to move or change text or pictures or to change the colours. These same skills will be needed when you want to *maintain* or *update* an existing Web site with the latest information and replacement pictures.

All editing must take place in the main page area of WebPlus, not in a Web browser such as Internet Explorer.

To start editing an existing Web site saved on your hard disc, click **Open Saved Site** from the WebPlus **Startup Wizard**. Alternatively you can select **File** and **Open...** from the WebPlus Menu Bar. The **Open** dialogue box appears as shown below.

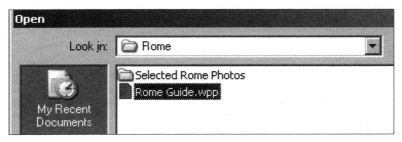

You will need to click the down arrow to the right of the **Look in:** bar shown above and then browse for the folder in which your Web site is saved. Now click **Open** as shown above and your Web site opens at the Home Page ready to start editing.

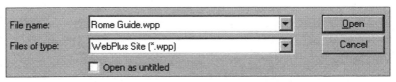

Selecting a Web Page for Editing

If you want to edit a particular page in a Web site, other than the Home Page, you need to make sure the page is selected in the **Site** panel in the WebPlus **Studio** as shown below. For example, to edit the page **Getting About Rome**, you need to double-click the entry for the page in the **Studio**, as shown below. The selected page opens ready for editing in the main page area of WebPlus.

The **Studio** panel on the right of the screen now displays the small eye icon next to the entry for **Getting About Rome**, showing that this is the Web page currently open for editing.

Editing a Master Page

To edit objects in the background layer, such as navigation bars, you will need to select and edit the appropriate *master page*. This can be done after clicking the **Site** tab in the **Studio** panel on the right of the WebPlus screen as shown above. Double-click the master page icon at the top of the **Site** panel, so that the eye icon appears next to it. Alternatively, use the **Page Locator** at the bottom left-hand side of the WebPlus screen.

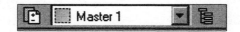

Editing Text

Select the text frame by clicking anywhere within it so that the eight small squares appear, as shown below.

Now select the text by dragging over it with the left mouse button held down. You can now apply any of the effects such as bold, italics, etc., and change the text font and size using the Text Toolbar across the top of the WebPlus screen, as shown below.

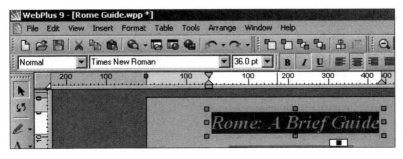

You can also delete text in a frame using the **Delete** and
Backspace keys and insert additional text by typing at the
cursor position.

Using the Attributes Tab to Change Colours, etc.

The **Attributes** tab on the right of the WebPlus screen
provides a quick and easy way to change the appearance of
a text frame. Make sure the text frame is selected and that
the text inside is also selected, then click the **Attributes** tab
shown below on the right.

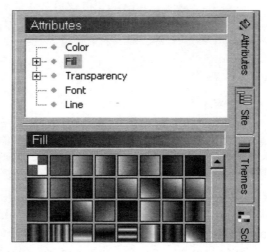

If you click **Color** shown above and then select a colour
from the palette below, any selected text in a frame will
change to the new colour. Similarly, if you select **Fill** as
shown above, then select a colour/pattern from the palette,
the background in the text frame will be filled with the new
colour/pattern. In a similar way, the **Attributes** feature in
WebPlus also allows you to change the text font and to
choose different types of line for the border of a text frame.

Editing Pictures

Before editing a picture it needs to be selected by clicking anywhere inside of the picture. Eight small squares appear.

Resizing a Picture

A selected picture can be resized by diagonally dragging one of the corner squares.

Moving a Picture

A picture can be moved about the page after placing the cursor over the picture. The cursor changes to a cross with four arrow heads. Keeping the left mouse button held down, drag the picture to the required position and then release the left button.

Cropping a Picture

The cropping operation removes surplus material around a picture or photograph while leaving the centre unchanged. It is similar to trimming with a guillotine. First select the picture by clicking over it so that the eight small squares appear. Then select the crop tool from the toolbar on the left-hand side of the Web Plus screen. When you move the cursor over any of the eight small squares, it changes to the shape of the crop tool shown on the right. If you drag any of the corner squares the picture is trimmed on all four sides. If you only want to crop one side of the picture, just drag the square in the middle of that side. If you make a mistake while cropping, you can either select **Edit** and **Undo** or click the **Undo** icon on the WebPlus toolbar. Alternatively use the crop tool, moving the cursor outwards to reverse the cropping operation.

Replacing a Picture

When a picture is selected in WebPlus, eight small squares appear around its perimeter. At the same time, the Picture Toolbar appears on the screen as shown below.

 The **Replace Picture** icon shown on the left of the toolbar makes it very easy to replace an existing selected picture in a Web page. Click the **Replace Picture** icon and the **Import Picture** dialogue box opens, allowing you to select a new picture from your hard disc.

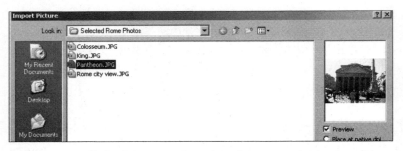

When you click the **Open** button, the new picture replaces the old one in the same size and position in the Web page.

The picture toolbar shown above also has icons for adjusting the brightness and contrast of a selected picture; there are also tools for changing the colours and size and resolution of a picture. The latter can have a significant effect on the speed with which a picture can be displayed on a Web browser.

The ChangeBar

The **ChangeBar** provides a very precise way of making changes to a selected screen object, such as a text frame or picture. If the **ChangeBar** is not visible, click its icon on the bottom right of the screen or select **View** and **ChangeBar** from the Menu Bar.

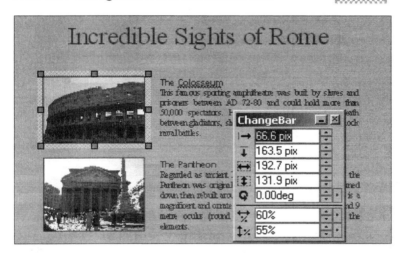

The **ChangeBar** pops up as shown above and allows you to make fine adjustments to the position and size of a selected text frame or picture. You can rotate a text frame or picture to any angle. In a selected text frame, you can change the font size, the spacing between lines of text and between letters and also set the text in columns. Changes are made by clicking the small arrows on the right of the **ChangeBar**.

After editing, the Web site should be saved again on the local hard disc as discussed earlier in this chapter.

Summary of the Work So Far

The work described in the last few chapters has shown how a Web site creation program like WebPlus can be used to:

- Create a Web site consisting of several pages, made up of text and pictures. WebPlus provides both ready-made templates and a blank canvas approach.

- Create a master page as a background layer to several Web pages.

- Include a navigation bar on a master page, enabling movement between Web pages and Web sites.

- Insert hyperlinks on Web pages and also insert multimedia objects such as sound and video clips.

- Use the **Preview** feature to view the site in a Web browser used by visitors to the site, such as Internet Explorer. Also to test that links and multimedia objects are functioning correctly.

- Edit Web pages during the creation of a new site or in the maintenance and updating of an existing site. This involves altering the content and format of text, replacing, resizing and cropping pictures and moving objects on the page. Also using the WebPlus **ChangeBar** to alter properties of text and screen objects, such as pictures.

Publishing a Web Site on the World Wide Web

All of the work so far has resulted in a Web site being saved on the hard disc inside of a local computer, i.e. a machine sitting in your home or office. The next stage is to *upload* the pages to a Web server so that they are accessible to a worldwide audience. This is discussed in the next chapter, **Publishing Your Web Site on the Internet**.

8

Publishing Your Web Site on the Internet

Introduction

The previous chapters have shown how you can use a program like WebPlus to create your own Web site. Initially the work is all carried out on your own computer and the pages are saved on your own hard disc. Then the new Web site is previewed in a Web browser such as Internet Explorer. (At this stage your Web site exists only on your own computer, not on the Internet). Any changes suggested by the preview are made by returning to the Web page creation program, such as WebPlus, where the text and pictures, etc., can be edited. When you are satisfied with your new Web site, the next task is to publish it on the Internet.

The main stages in publishing a Web site are:

- Obtaining a unique address for your Web site.
- Choosing a Web host to provide space for your site
- Transferring or *uploading* your site to the Web host
- Maintaining your Web site
- Promoting your site to other Web users.

Obtaining a Web Address or URL

Personal Web addresses usually start with the letters **www.**, short for World Wide Web. The complete address of a Web site is known as a *URL* or *Uniform Resource Locator*. The letters after **www.** are known as the *domain name*.

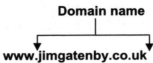

Domain name

www.jimgatenby.co.uk

Visitors can connect to your Web site by typing the URL into the address bar of a Web browser such as Internet Explorer.

The domain name can be either your name or a name you make up. Domain names have to be registered and you may find that your chosen name has already been taken, especially if it uses an extension such as **.co.uk**, for example. You may still be able to use your chosen name but with a different *extension*. The first part of the extension indicates the *type* of Web site, for example:

com	Commercial organization
co	UK commercial organisation
net	Internet Service
org	Non-profit organization

Some newer domain types for worldwide use include:

biz	available for businesses
info	information oriented sites
name	personal site used by an individual

The domain name can end with a *country code*, such as:

au	Australia	**uk**	United Kingdom
fr	France	**es**	Spain

The cost of registering a domain name may be included in the cost of a Web hosting package, as discussed shortly. Alternatively you can find lots of companies who will register your domain name, typically for £2-£3 per year, but more for certain domain types. Enter the keywords **domain names** into a search engine such as Google to find companies offering help with domain registration, such as:

www.ukreg.com

www.123domainnames.co.uk

www.register.com

The domain name may also be used in a more personal e-mail address such as:

jimsmith@jimswebsite.co.uk

Nominet UK

This is the official registry for domain names ending in **.uk**. Registering a domain name is normally done through a registration agent such as a Web host, an Internet Service Provider or a company specialising in the registration of domain names. Nominet offer a free service called WHOIS which allows you to find out if a particular domain name is still available. There is a link to WHOIS on:

http://www.nominet.org.uk

Web Hosts

A Web host is a company providing space on their computers (known as *servers*) to store your Web site. They may also provide you with a *domain name* such as:

myownwebsite.co.uk

The domain name may be free, as part of a monthly Web hosting package. Alternatively, if you have already registered your own domain name, this may be transferred to a new account with a Web host.

If you subscribe to an Internet Service Provider such as AOL, they will probably allocate some Web space to you – typically about 2 MB – enough to store a small Web site. A larger personal Web site may need up to about 10MB. If you are running a business or professional site and your Web site is likely to grow, you will probably need to consider a *hosting* package costing a few pounds a month. You can find out more by entering the keywords **web hosts** into a search engine such as Google.

Web hosts generally offer a range of packages, often starting with free Web space and then increasing in price, typically from £2-£30 per month and more for larger company sites. If you choose one of the free Web hosting options you will probably need to accept a rather unwieldy domain name such as:

members.myownwebsite.superhost.uk.net

To have a (relatively) simple and more memorable domain name such as **bbc.co.uk**, you will need to sign up for one of the packages requiring a monthly or annual subscription.

You may also need to consider how much *bandwidth* (or data transfer) the host can provide per month. This is a measure of the amount of "traffic" visiting your site.

Some Web hosts, such as 1&1 and Yahoo! GeoCities provide Web creation tools and ready-made templates which can be adapted to make your own personal Web site. For businesses there are Web hosts providing statistics on the number of visitors to a site and "plug-in" features such as shopping carts and online payment facilities.

Essential Information Provided by a Web Host

The Web host (which may be your Internet Service Provider, such as AOL) will arrange a **username** and **password** with you and provide an **FTP Address** (such as **ftp.superhost.uk.net**), for example. This information will be needed when you upload your site to the Web host's server. The Web host should also provide instructions for this task. Web site creation programs like WebPlus and Microsoft FrontPage have a built-in FTP (File Transfer Protocol) program for uploading Web sites to Web hosts' servers. Otherwise a special *FTP client* program is used. This topic is discussed later in this chapter.

Criteria for Choosing a Web Host

The computing magazines regularly carry advertisements and comparisons of the Web hosting companies. Some of the criteria to be considered when choosing a Web host are:

- The monthly fee and initial set up fee (if any)
- The cost of domain name registration (if any)
- The use of simple, easy-to-remember domain names
- The amount of Web space provided
- E-mail facilities provided
- The bandwith or data transfer rate, i.e. the amount of traffic (visitors) allowed per month
- The reliability of the service.

Uploading Web Pages to the Internet

The next few pages show how a Web site can be uploaded to the Internet. In this example, the Serif WebPlus Web site creation program is used. This has a built-in FTP facility which makes the uploading of a Web site very easy.

From the WebPlus Menu Bar select **Help** and **Get Web Space**. This connects to the Serif Web site displaying an offer of **Free Web Space for WebPlus 9 Owners!** as shown below.

Clicking the **Free Web Space** link shown above connects to the *SPEEDY.UK.NET* site with details of their packages for WebPlus 9 users. The free Web space offer includes 25MB of Web space, more than enough space for a small personal Web site; the free offer is limited to 30 days but this is ample time for you to become fully conversant with the task of publishing your Web site on the Internet. To continue after 30 days you can purchase a discounted *SPEEDY.UK.NET* **Starter Hosting** package costing £39.99 a year.

The free Web hosting package gives you a Web address of the type **www.yourname.speedynet.uk.net**, whereas the subscription packages allow a simpler form such as **www.yourname.co.uk**.

Signing Up For a Web Package

Having selected a package such as **Free Trial** or **Starter Hosting**, click the **Continue** button to start the process of signing up to a *SPEEDY.UK.NET* account. This is simply a case of entering your personal details such as **Name, Email Address** and **Phone Number**. This is also the point where you make up and enter your **Username** and **Password** (twice).

Username
Please choose a username for your account
Your website domain name will be
http://www.USERNAME.speedy.uk.net, with
USERNAME replaced with the username you
enter here.

Password
Enter your password in both boxes opposite
(continuity verification)

The **Username** entered above becomes part of your Web address, i.e. **http://www.USERNAME.speedy.uk.net**. After clicking **Continue**, the next screen **Signup Complete!** presents the full details of your new account.

The following information is essential for uploading files to the Internet:

FTP Address: for example **ftp.speedy.uk.net**

Username: (created by the user as shown above)

Password: (created by the user as shown above)

The **Signup Complete!** screen just discussed also includes a link to the *SPEEDY.UK.NET* **Account Portal**. This can also be accessed at any time from the Web site at **www.speedy.uk.net**, by entering your **Username** and **Password**, as set up in the sign-up process just discussed. This shows the type of account you have signed up for and the amount of storage used and available, as shown below.

At this stage, no Web site has been uploaded so the **Website Storage** bar shown above is empty and there are still 30 days left on the free trial. There is also a link, **View my settings** which allows you to print out a copy of all your details, **Username, Password, Web address** and **FTP address**. There are no mailboxes provided in the free Web hosting package used in this example.

There is a useful support section, **Uploading Pages**, accessed via a link on the **Account Portal** of *SPEEDY.UK.NET*. This gives very clear instructions on uploading Web pages from your computer to a *SPEEDY.UK.NET* Web server.

As shown above, help is given for various methods of uploading Web pages:

Serif WebPlus 9

This involves uploading a Web site using **File** and **Publish Site** in WebPlus 9 to upload a site created in WebPlus 9. This method is discussed in the next few pages.

BulletProof FTP and CuteFTP

These are dedicated file transfer programs which can be used to upload Web sites which have been created in a variety of ways and saved in the HTML format.

Uploading a WebSite from Serif WebPlus

Before starting work you will need from your Web host your **Username**, **Password** and the address of their FTP server, such as **ftp://ftp.speedy.uk.net**.

Open the required Web site in WebPlus, then click **File** and **Publish Site** from the Menu Bar, as shown below.

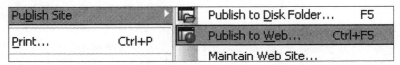

Then click **Publish to Web...** as shown above. Alternatively, click the **Publish to Web** icon, shown on the right, on the **Standard Toolbar** across the top of the WebPlus screen. The first time you use WebPlus to publish a site on the Internet, you are presented with the **Account Details** dialogue box shown below.

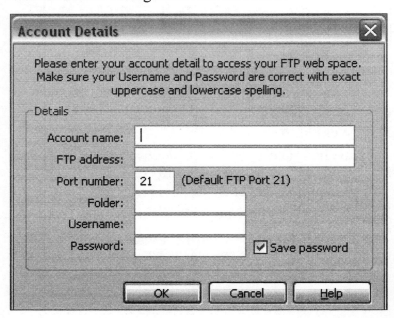

In the **Account Details** box on the previous page, make up and enter an **Account name** to identify this particular account; for example, **My Speedy.uk.net Account**. It's possible for you to have more than one hosting account.

In the **FTP address** box enter the address of your Web host's FTP server, such as **ftp://ftp.speedy.uk.net**.

Unless supplied with alternative information by your Web host, leave the **Port number** set at **21** and leave **Folder** blank. Finally enter the **Username** and **Password** that you arranged with your Web host. Click the **Save password** box so that you don't need to enter the password on future uploads.

Now click the **OK** button as shown on the previous page and the **Publish To Web** dialogue box opens as shown below.

In the **Publish to Web** dialogue box on the previous page, if you have more than one Web hosting account, this can be selected from the drop-down menu launched by clicking the down-arrow next to the **FTP Account** bar. You can also add a new account, by clicking the **Add** button shown on the previous page. This launches the **Account Details** dialogue box shown earlier. The **Publish to Web** dialogue box also allows you to **Edit** or **Delete** a Web hosting account. Finally enter your **Username** and **Password**, if they were not infilled automatically.

Now click the **Upload** button and your computer should connect to the Web host's server and upload the files making up your Web site. If you have published this site before, you can select an **incremental update** in which only files that have changed since the last upload will be copied to the host's server. Otherwise click **No** to **upload all files**.

With a small site and a broadband connection, the upload only takes a few seconds and you are informed that the upload was successful.

Viewing Your Own Web Site Online

Your Web site is now installed on the World Wide Web and you will shortly be able to see your site "online" for the first time. Enter the Web address (or "URL") of your new site, such as **http://www.myownwebsite.co.uk**, into your Web browser such as Internet Explorer as shown below. (Your Web host will let you know your Web address – it will probably include your **Username**.)

Your Web site opens up in your Web browser on the Internet. If you have been able to complete all of the work in this book, you should now be able to:

- Move around the pages of your site using a navigation bar.

- Click any hyperlinks and move to other Web pages or to other Web sites.

- Click a "thumbnail" image to see a full-page view.

- Launch an animation, multi-media clip containing sound or video or an "animated marquee" of text scrolling across the Web page.

- Send yourself an automatically addressed e-mail from a link built into your Web site.

Maintaining Your Web Site

From time to time you will need to make alterations to your Web site. These may include regular updates with the latest information, such as news and recently planned events. Or you might want to replace some photographs with improved, later editions.

The general method is to return to your Web creation program such as WebPlus and open up the Web site files stored on your local hard disc. Then make any necessary alterations to the text, pictures, multimedia clips, etc., as discussed earlier in the chapter **Previewing and Editing a Web Site**.

Preview the site, still working only on your local computer, before making any final amendments and saving the site on your local hard disc.

Now click **File** and **Publish to Web...** or click the **Publish to Web** icon shown on the right. Since the site has been published before, WebPlus only displays the **Publish to Web** dialogue box shown earlier. Make sure your **Username** and **Password** are entered correctly and then it is only a case of clicking **Upload** to publish your updated site.

After connecting to the remote server of your Web host, you are asked if you want to perform an **incremental update**, i.e. uploading only the files that have changed.

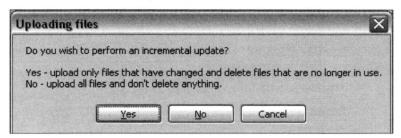

If you click the **Yes** button shown above you should quickly be informed that the upload was successful.

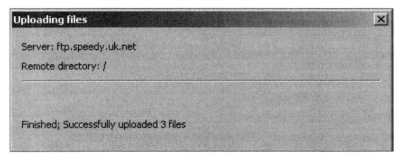

In this example of an incremental update, only 3 updated files had to be uploaded, compared with 14 when the whole site was initially published to the Web.

WebPlus has a Maintenance feature accessed by selecting **File**, **Publish Site** and **Maintain Web Site....** Then click the **Maintain** button on the **Maintain Web Site** dialogue which appears. The **Maintain Web Site** window is then displayed. This is similar to the Windows Explorer and allows you to carry out tasks such as deleting and renaming files and folders, etc., from your Web site.

FTP

A Web site is *uploaded*, i.e. copied, to an Internet Web server, using a system called FTP or File Transfer Protocol. Web creation programs like Serif WebPlus and Microsoft FrontPage have a built-in FTP facility which simplifies the uploading of Web sites. Alternatively, there are several dedicated FTP programs, known as FTP clients, such as:

BulletProof FTP	**(www.bpftp.com)**
CuteFTP	**(www.cuteftp.com)**
WS_FTP	**(www.ipswitch.com)**

If you log on to any of the above Web sites you will probably be able to download a free (but time-limited) version of the software or buy an unrestricted version.

BulletProof FTP Client

Transfer Files with BulletProof Reliability!

<u>Buy Now: $29.95 USD</u> :: <u>Download Trial (1.23 MB)</u>

Overview

Need to upload your website? Or trade files?

BulletProof FTP is a fully automated FTP client, with many advanced fe resuming, leech mode, ftp search and much more. Perfect for person: Software and Music traders.

Download files in any order, from any directory on an FTP site.

Automatically reconnect and resume from where it left off if the for a specified period of time. This works with uploading as well!

Browse the FTP site from the cache while off line or transferring - the FTP server like other FTP clients.

Downloading a Free Copy of CuteFTP

This is a popular program for transferring files both to and from Web servers. You can download a free (30-day) copy of the software from the GlobalSCAPE Web site at:

www.cuteftp.com

There are links on the site for both **Home** and **Professional** versions. Clicking one of these leads to a page describing CuteFTP and including buttons to either **Buy Now** or **Download**. Clicking **Download** displays a box requiring you to select a language and supply your e-mail address.

Now click **Submit** and **Download Now** and you are asked to choose a folder (or accept the default folder offered) in which to save the file to be downloaded, **cuteftp.exe**.

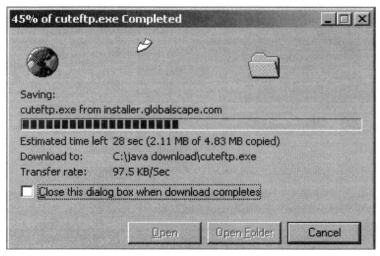

When the download is complete, you only need to click **Run** a couple of times and then click **Next** before **CuteFTP** is installed on your computer and ready to use.

Using CuteFTP

When you launch CuteFTP from **Start, All Programs, CuteFTP,** you have to fill in the details of your Web host. This can be done using the **CuteFTP Connection Wizard** or by entering the details straight into a single dialogue box. The Connection Wizard can be started by selecting **File, Connect** and **Connection Wizard....**

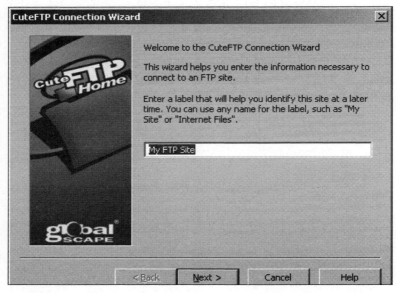

First you have to give your new site a name or **Label.** Then it is just a case of clicking **Next** and entering the following information – which is required when making any FTP connection for the first time.

Host Address: e.g. **ftp://ftp.speedy.uk.net**

Username: (arranged with your Web host)

Password: (arranged with your Web host).

You will also need to enter the path to the folder on your hard disc where your Web pages and any associated pictures are stored, for example:

C:\All Web Sites\ Rome

Instead of using the **Wizard**, you can connect more directly by selecting **File, Connect** and **Connect** (again). The following dialogue box appears, again requiring the usual information necessary to connect to an FTP server.

After completing the **Site Properties** dialogue box shown above, click **Connect** and you are connected to the host server, with a Windows Explorer-like interface as shown on the next page.

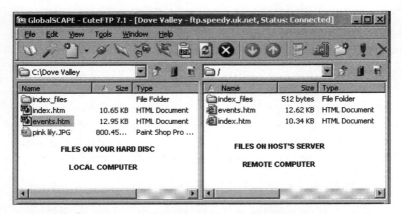

You may need to browse to find the folder (on your hard disc), containing your Web pages and any necessary pictures. These are shown in the left-hand panel above. Browsing is carried out after clicking the down arrow, shown to the right of **C:\Dove Valley** in the above example.

You must make sure you are connected to the Web host's computer, as discussed earlier, by using one of the connection methods off **File** and **Connect**. This shown by **Status: Connected** at the top right of the CuteFTP window shown above.

Transferring Files to the Web Host

Uploading of files is carried out by simply dragging the required files from the left-hand panel to the right.

Maintaining a Web Site in CuteFTP

When it is necessary to update any of the pages of your Web site, return to your Web page creation program and carry out any changes. Then save the modified Web pages in the same folder as before. Start up CuteFTP and connect to your Web host. Then drag and drop the modified files from the left-hand panel to the right, as before.

Attracting Visitors to Your Web Site

A Web site may be created for a variety of purposes. You may wish to share news, information and pictures with friends, relatives or people sharing a common interest or hobby. Alternatively, you might want to advertise a small business you are starting up. Whatever the purpose of your site, you'll probably want it to be viewed by as wide an audience as possible.

Once your site is up and running, visitors are likely to arrive from various sources:

- People who type the URL of your site into the **Address** bar of a Web browser, such as Internet Explorer, shown below.

- Surfers who finish up at your Web site after clicking a link on another Web site.

- People who have entered key words into a *search engine* such as Google, or after clicking **Search** in a Web browser like Internet Explorer.

Publicising Your Web Address (URL)

Your Web address could be included in all of your e-mails as a clickable hyperlink, as discussed earlier in this book. You could send an e-mail to all of your friends, relatives, contacts, etc., and ask them to view your Web site and add it to their list of favourite sites, i.e. bookmark it in their Web browser. Your URL might also be displayed on all of your business cards, stationery and any advertisements.

Links From Other Web Sites

Web sites are rated highly if a lot of other sites link to them; this means they will be placed higher in the list of results from a search in Google, for example. So, if your site is about, say, the Russian Blue (a breed of cat), you could contact other relevant cat Web sites to arrange mutual links. This should increase the number of visitors to all of the linked sites and also increase the amount of information available to the Web surfer.

Finding Your Site as a Result of a Search

There are other strategies to improve your site's chances of being placed near the top of the list of results of a keyword search in a program such as Google. To help your site to be prominent in the results of a search, you might try the following techniques:

- Register your site with the well-known search programs, such as Google, Yahoo and Ask (Jeeves).
- Include relevant keywords in your Web pages. These should be in the title, near the top of the page and also scattered frequently throughout the pages.

For more help and information have a look at:

htttp://searchenginewatch.com

Working with Photographs

Introduction

Photographs are an essential part of many Web sites, especially if a site involves family and friends or, for example, the promotion of a small business. The development of relatively cheap digital cameras has made it very easy for anyone to create good quality pictures without being a highly skilled photographer. If necessary, photographs can appear on a Web site within minutes of being taken.

A very satisfactory digital camera can be obtained for under £100, although it's possible to pay much more if you intend to work at a professional level. When you buy a digital camera the box usually contains a cable to connect the camera to a USB port on your computer.

The USB ports are small rectangular slots on the front or back of the computer. The  digital camera package may also include a CD containing software to handle the copying of images from your camera onto the computer's hard disc. Microsoft Windows contains The Microsoft Scanner and Camera Wizard for this purpose.

Digital Editing

Digital editing software may be supplied with a new camera. This allows a photograph to be polished up by adjusting properties such as the brightness and contrast or cropping to remove unwanted areas. There are lots of modestly-priced digital editing packages such as Adobe PhotoShop Elements and Corel Paint Shop Pro (shown below) which can be used to add the finishing touches to your photographs. These programs are easy to use and often have a "single click" feature for automatically improving the general quality of a photograph.

Scanning Photographic Prints

Old photographs, even if they are quite tatty, can be scanned and stored on your computer. A digital editing program can be used to remove scratches from an old print.

Anyone who uses a traditional film camera to produce glossy prints can also use a scanner to enjoy the many benefits of digital photography. Once images are safely stored on your hard disc they can be enhanced in a digital image editing program like Paint Shop Pro or Adobe Photoshop Elements. Various scanning tasks can be carried out on photographs (and also other documents) up to A4 size and include:

- Saving a photograph in a folder of your choice.
- Importing a photo into a digital editing program.
- Sending a photograph to a Web site.
- Sending a photograph to be included with an e-mail message, as an attachment.

Organising Your Photographs in Folders

All of the photographs needed for the Rome Web site, discussed earlier, were saved in a newly-created **Rome** folder, **C:\Photos 2005\Rome**, as shown below.

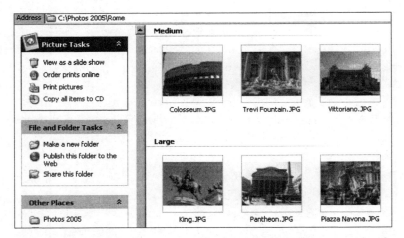

The photographs above are displayed as **Thumbnails** in the Windows Explorer. The **Thumbnails** option is selected from the **View** menu in Explorer. The menus down the left-hand side can be displayed by selecting **View**, **Explorer Bar** and clicking **Folders** to remove the tick.

More help on creating and viewing folders in the Windows Explorer is given in my book, Computing for the Older Generation from Bernard Babani (publishing) Ltd.

File Formats

Two of the most popular formats for saving pictures for use on the Internet are the JPEG and the GIF. The JPEG (or JPG) format is most popular for saving photographs whereas the GIF is often used for photographs, drawings and artwork with not too many colours.

The JPEG File Format

Please note in the previous screenshot that all of the photographs have the extension **.JPG** at the end of the file name, as in **King.JPG**. The **.JPG** file name extension refers to the way the photograph was saved after it was copied from the digital camera. **.JPG** is short for the **JPEG** file format, an

King.JPG

acronym for Joint Photographic Experts Group. The **JPEG** format is a popular way of saving photographs on a disc; the files are compressed so that they take up less disc space, while still maintaining an acceptable quality.

Photographic files can be extremely bulky. This makes them very slow to copy across the Internet, for example when you are publishing pages to your Web site. Also when visitors to your site are downloading your Web pages to view on their computer.

If someone is browsing the Internet and their computer appears to hang up because Web pages are very slow to load, they will probably give up and look at a different site. So it's a good idea to try to reduce the size of your JPEG photo files if possible.

You can check the size of your photographs in the Windows Explorer by selecting **View** and **Details** as shown below. As can be seen below, a photograph can be very large indeed; too large in fact to fit on a single floppy disc, a common storage medium until the last few years.

King.JPG	1,121 KB	Paint Shop Pro X Im...
Pantheon.JPG	1,157 KB	Paint Shop Pro X Im...
Piazza Navona.JPG	1,463 KB	Paint Shop Pro X Im...
Cameraman.JPG	1,341 KB	Paint Shop Pro X Im...

Reducing the Size of a Photograph

Photographs can take up a huge amount of disc storage space and can be slow to transfer around the Internet. There are several ways to reduce the size of your images, as discussed below. This will make your site more attractive to visitors, since they won't have to wait as long for pages to be downloaded to their computer.

Resizing

An image can be scaled down in an image editing program, as discussed shortly, reducing the size of the JPEG file saved on disc.

Cropping

This involves trimming unwanted areas from around the outside of the image, producing a smaller file size.

Saving in a Compressed Format

When you save a photograph in the JPEG file format discussed earlier, you can reduce the file size by increasing the amount of compression. Compression is a process by which unnecessary detail is removed from a picture while maintaining a reasonable quality.

Thumbnail

Some programs, such as Microsoft FrontPage, allow you to save a *thumbnail*, i.e. a miniature version of an image, on a Web page. The thumbnail loads faster than the full size image. The thumbnail is set up as a clickable link to the full size picture, with an explanatory note on the screen.

The above topics are discussed in more detail on the pages which follow.

Resizing an Image in Paint

You can resize an image by loading it into the **Paint** program supplied with Microsoft Windows. Then select **Image** and **Stretch/Skew...**, as shown below.

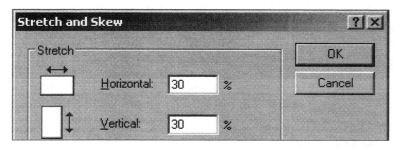

After scaling the picture down by a suitable factor such as 30%, for example, the image is saved as a JPEG file. The new file will be considerably reduced and should be much faster when transferred across the Internet.

Cropping an Image in the Paint Program

In the **Rome** folder mentioned earlier, there is a photograph of one of the "living statues" in the Piazza Navona. The file name of the photo is **Cameraman.JPG** and it is shown below displayed as a thumbnail in the Windows Explorer. Allowing the cursor to hover over the file thumbnail causes a small information window to pop up, as shown on the right below. You can see that the image has a resolution of **2816 x 2112** pixels and a size of **1.30MB**.

Dimensions: 2816 x 2112
Date Picture Taken: 18/10/2005 10:42
Camera Model: X-3,C-60Z
Type: Paint Shop Pro X Image
Size: 1.30 MB

The image is shown below, loaded into the Windows **Paint** program using **File** and **Open**.... The **Paint** selection tool was used to outline the rectangle enclosing the required area of the photograph.

The selected area is then placed on the Windows clipboard using **Edit** and **Copy** from the **Paint** Menu Bar. (The clipboard is a temporary storage area for text and pictures). A new blank window is opened in **Paint** and the cropped image pasted from the clipboard onto the **Paint** window, using **Edit** and **Paste**, as shown on the next page.

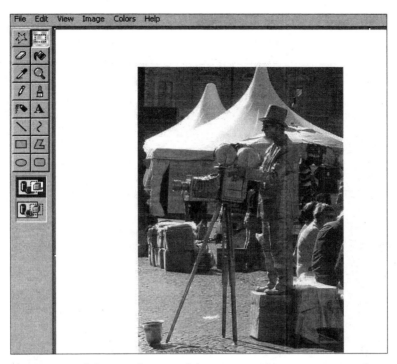

The cropped image is saved in **Paint** using a name such as **Cameraman2.JPG**. Please note that by changing the name of the image file to **Cameraman2.JPG**, the original copy of the image **Cameraman.JPG** is preserved on the disc, in case it is needed in the future. If you now allow the cursor to hover over the thumbnail of the image in the Windows Explorer, you find the file size has decreased substantially.

Cameraman2.JPG

Dimensions: 845 x 634
Type: Paint Shop Pro X Image
Size: 36.9 KB

Cropping in Paint Shop Pro

The original **Cameraman.JPG** file is shown again below, opened in the popular digital editing program Paint Shop Pro. When the cropping tool (shown on the right) is selected, a suggested cropped area appears, highlighted in a rectangular border with eight small squares on the perimeter. The area to remain after cropping can be adjusted by dragging the squares.

If you now double-click inside of the highlighted area, all of the material around the outside is removed. The cropped file can then be saved using **File** and **Save As...**. This time I used the new file name **Cameraman3.JPG** to avoid wiping out any of the earlier versions of the file.

Saving Images with Increased Compression

When you save a photographic image as a JPEG file in a program such as Paint Shop Pro or Photoshop Elements, there is an option to increase the *compression*. In Paint Shop Pro select **File** and **Save As...** then **Options....**

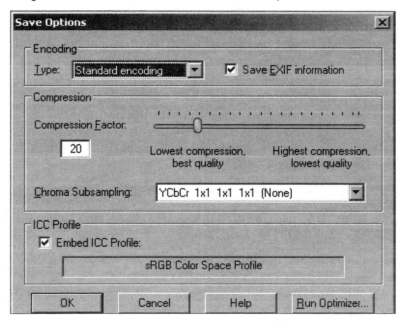

In the **Save Options** dialogue box above, the **Compression Factor** slider can be dragged along the horizontal bar. Moving the slider to the right gives higher compression and lower quality, making the photographic image smaller and therefore faster to load in a Web browser.

To make sure the original, uncompressed version of the photograph is not overwritten on the hard disc, enter a new **File name** for the compressed version in the **Save As** dialogue box and click the **Save** button.

Online Photo Albums

One of the easiest ways to display your latest photographs is to sign up to one of the many online photo albums – these give you some Web space, your own Web address and quite a lot more besides. They are an excellent way of looking at your photos and then perhaps carrying out some editing. Some of the online photo albums also enable you to purchase prints online. This may be easier and cheaper than going to your local store.

Creating a photo album online is really just a matter of signing up with a username and password, followed by the uploading of your pictures as files from your hard disc. In most cases, it costs nothing to do this. However, paying for a premium account will give you more features and extra storage space for your photographs; a premium account album will not display adverts, which pop up unexpectedly and can be annoying when you are trying to concentrate.

Online photo albums can interact with mobile phones so that images may be transferred between them. Tiny camera-phone pictures are easier to see and can be edited and enhanced on the computer screen before printing. Photographs can be sent from your album to other sites such as eBay or to an online diary or journal such as Blogger, discussed in Chapter 2. So the online photo album is a versatile medium which can interact with a number of different Internet services.

Once your friends and family know the Web address of your online album, they can easily share your photographs, which may be displayed as a slideshow at the click of a mouse.

There are lots of Web sites providing online photo albums. To have a look at some of the latest and most popular, type keywords like **online photo albums** into a search engine such as Google. Some typical results are shown below.

Photobucket.com

As you can see above, **www.photobucket.com** is near the top of the results and in a Google search this indicates that it's a much-visited and popular site. The next few pages look at **Photobucket.com** in more detail.

Once you have logged on to the **www.photobucket.com** address, it is just a case of signing up so that you can become a user. Simply click **Sign Up Free Now!** or click **Join Now!** A registration form appears, requiring details such as your first and last names, username, password, date of birth, postcode, e-mail address, etc.

Get your own Photobucket account

All fields required

* First Name	
* Last Name	
* Username	- Used to identify your album -
* Password	- Must be at least 5 characters -
* Valid Email	Email policy
* Birthdate	Month ▼ Day ▼ Year ▼

As shown above, you need to make up a **Username** and **Password** so that you can sign on and manage your photo album in the future. Once the registration form has been completed, you have a free account with Photobucket. A page of advertisements from other companies then appears (e.g. earn cash at home, registering for eBay, etc.) Log in with your **Username** and **Password**. Next the **Photobucket Home** page is displayed, ready for uploading your latest photographs to the Internet.

As shown below in the extract from the **Photobucket Home** page you can submit a single picture or a set of several pictures.

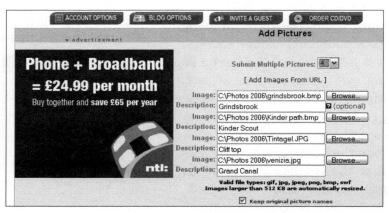

In the dialogue box on the previous page click **Browse...** to start searching for the pictures from the folders on your hard disc. After selecting the required photo, click **Open** and the file location will appear next to **Image**, as shown below.

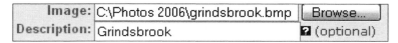

When all of the pictures have been selected, click the **Submit** button. This will upload the images to the online photo album and will take a few minutes. Notice that any pictures greater than **512 KB** in size are automatically resized. The uploaded photos appear in the lower half of the **Photobucket home** page.

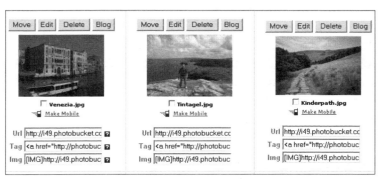

Once the pictures are safely uploaded to the online photo album you may wish to make some changes, using the small menu which appears above each image. **Move** allows you to transfer the image to another album. Additional albums are created using the **Add Sub Album** box on the **Photobucket Home** page as shown below.

In the photo album on the previous page, if you want to move the Venice picture to a sub album **Italy,** for example, click **Move** from the small menu above the picture.

Click **Move** again from the **Move Pictures** window which appears, as shown below, to move the picture to the selected sub folder, **Italy** in this example.

The **Edit** option shown in the top screenshot allows you to add a description to the photo, as shown on the right. It's also possible to resize and rotate the picture. Click the **Delete** button to remove an image.

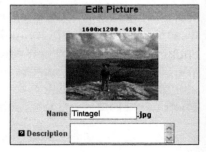

Posting a Photo to a Blog

This option in **Photobucket** allows your photo to be posted to an online journal such as **Blogger.** To do this, you need to tell **Photobucket** which blogging program you use. At the top of the **Photobucket Home** page, select **BLOG OPTIONS**, then choose your blog program from the drop-down menu which appears.

After choosing your blogging program, enter your blogging username and password. Select your blog and then return to the album. Click **Blog** above the image, and then **Post Entry** in the screen which follows. If you now log on to your blog, the new picture will appear on the page.

Sharing Photos with Friends and Family

To ensure that friends and family can view your photos, you need to set the **ACCOUNT OPTIONS** on the menu at the top of the **Home** page.

Select **ACCOUNT OPTIONS** and you will see **Album Options** in the lower half of the page. The **Make public** option can be set by clicking **Yes** or **No.** Here you can choose who may view the photo album – the general public or just your friends. You can limit viewing to just your friends by clicking **No**, then giving a read only password, which will allow only selected people access to your photos.

So if a friend wished to see your latest holiday snaps, they would visit the Web site at **www.photobucket.com**, type in your username followed by their read-only password. This password is unique to them and is different from your own.

As you can see below, a friend has logged in to a photo album as shown by the message ***Logged in read only.** They can view it but not make any changes.

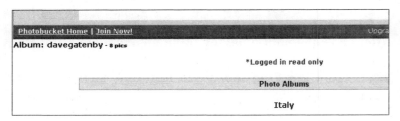

Showing Your Album as a Slideshow

Online photograph albums enable you to share pictures with your friends and family wherever they are in the world. With **Photobucket**, the album can be presented in the form of a slideshow. Click **SLIDESHOW** in the **Home** page and your photos will be displayed automatically.

It's possible to change the length of the time interval between each picture showing.

Index

SERIF WEBPLUS 9 READER OFFER

Serif offers readers the chance to save £10 off the latest version of WebPlus.

Purchase WebPlus 9 for £49.99* (List price £59.99)
Save £10!

Package includes: Program CD, Resource CD & Manual
*Excludes £3 shipping & handling charge

WebPlus 9 is the easy-to-use Web package that breaks down the technical barriers and allows users to create professional looking sites. The program's fantastic range of features includes:

DTP Style Page Layout – makes it easy to design truly outstanding Web pages
Integrated Layout Checker – a helping hand to remedy common layout problems
Built-in Site Maintenance – update your site after it's published to the Web
HTML Import – import text and graphics from existing Web pages
Amazing Filter Effects – add stunning textures and 3D effects to your pages

To purchase WebPlus 9 for the special price of £49.99* call Serif now on: **0800 376 1981 (UK Freephone)** quoting code: **RO/BABANI/WP9/0406**

or complete the following form and post it with your payment details to: **Babani WebPlus offer, Serif (Europe) Ltd, PO Box 2000, Nottingham, NG11 8BR**

IMPORTANT NOTE

The author and publishers of this book accept no responsibility for the supply, quality or magnetic contents of the compact discs, or in respect of any damage or injury that might be suffered or caused by their use. This offer may be subject to alteration or withdrawal without further notice.

Serif WebPlus 9 Discount Order Form
Payment Information

Title [   ] Initials [   ] Surname [   ]

Address [

          Postcode   Email   ]

Daytime Telephone Number _____

Email address _____

Product	Quantity	Sub Total	Total inc. £3.00 S&H.
Serif WebPlus 9 (£49.99) (includes Program CD, Resource CD & Manual)			

I enclose a crossed cheque/Postal Order made payable to Serif (Europe) Ltd for: £_____

Or please debit my ☐ Switch ☐ Mastercard ☐ Visa

Card No:_____ Valid From:_____

Issue No:_____ Expires: _____

Signature:_____

Rights and Restrictions: Offer available to UK residents only. Please allow up to 28 days for delivery. Data Protection Act 1998: Information you supply Serif may be used to provide you with details about carefully targeted customer offers. Serif may also share information with relevant third parties. Please tick the box if you do not want to be contacted by Serif ☐ or third parties ☐ for these purposes.

Marketing Code: RO/BABANI/WP9/0406